# Vocabulary in the Elementary and Middle School

### Dale D. Johnson

*Louisiana Tech University*

### *Allyn and Bacon*

*Boston • London • Toronto • Sydney • Tokyo • Singapore*

**Series Editor:** *Arnis E. Burvikovs*
**Editor in Chief, Education:** *Paul A. Smith*
**Editorial Assistant:** *Patrice Mailloux*
**Marketing Manager:** *Jackie Aaron*
**Editorial-Production Coordinator:** *Marla Feuerstein*
**Composition Buyer:** *Linda Cox*
**Electronic Composition:** *Peggy Cabot, Cabot Computer Services*
**Manufacturing Buyer:** *Julie McNeill*
**Cover Designer:** *Brian Gogolin*

*Library of Congress Cataloging-in-Publication Data*

Johnson, Dale D.
    Vocabulary in the elementary and middle school / Dale D. Johnson
      p.  cm.
    Includes bibliographical references and index.
    ISBN 0-205-29862-1
      1. Vocabulary—Study and teaching.  2. Language arts.  I. Title.
LB1574.5 .J64 2000
372.44—dc21                               00-040135
                                                CIP

Printed in the United States of America

10  9  8  7  6  5  4  3  2  1       05  04  03  02  01  00

*A person who has a loyal best friend, an energetic, gifted, and inspiring colleague, a valued sidekick, or an abiding love—that person is saturated with good fortune. To realize all those qualities in the person to whom you have been joyously wed for fifteen years is the ultimate in felicity. I dedicate this book to my wife, Bonnie, with love and gratitude. She always will be number one in my book.*

# Contents

# *Preface*

Published in 1998 under the sponsorship of the Commission on Behavioral and Social Sciences Education of the National Research Council, *Preventing Reading Difficulties in Young Children* generated intense interest both before and after its publication. Most classroom teachers and literacy educators rejoiced in this publication of the Council's findings and recommendations. The book, edited by Catherine E. Snow, M. Susan Burns, and Peg Griffin, was researched and prepared by the Committee on the Prevention of Reading Difficulties in young children. This committee included in its membership a virtual "who's who" of respected researchers in language, literacy, and cognitive psychology, including Marilyn Jager Adams, Edward J. Kame'enui, William Labov, Annemarie Sullivan Palincsar, Charles Perfetti, Keith Stanovich, Dorothy Strickland, and Elizabeth Sulzby. One of the findings of the committee is of particular relevance to this book:

> Several factors have been shown to promote comprehension: vocabulary, including full and precise understanding of the meanings of words; background knowledge about the subject matter; familiarity with semantic and syntactic structures that signal meaningful relationships among the words; appreciation of the writing conventions used to achieve different communicative purposes (e.g., irony, humor); verbal reasoning ability, which permits inferences to be made by reading between the lines; and verbal memory capacity.
>
> Comprehension can be enhanced through instruction that is focused on concept and vocabulary growth and the syntax and rhetorical structures of written language, as well as through experience gained by reading both independently and interactively in dyads or groups. (pp. 321–322)

Indeed, vocabulary plays a critical role in reading comprehension, but vocabulary is crucial to much more in communication than reading.

I have recommended several works to my readers throughout the book, but a few merit special prominence:

*The Lexicon in Acquisition* (E. Clark, 1993), which synthesizes careful research about how young children acquire and build a lexicon.

*Words in the Mind: An Introduction to the Mental Lexicon* (J. Aitchison, 1994), which illuminates empirical and theoretical findings about the mental lexicon.

*The Language Instinct: How the Mind Creates Language* (S. Pinker, 1994), which describes engrossing research about how young children acquire language.

*The Cambridge Encyclopedia of the English Language* (D. Crystal, 1995), which presents invaluable information on semantics and the English lexicon.

*The Science of Words* (G. Miller, 1996), which documents that a scientific approach can result in insights and truths about words and their acquisition.

*Word Works: Exploring Language Play* (B. Johnson, 1999), which radiates the joy and excitement that are the rewards of those who play with words and language.

I learned much from these books while doing research for mine. I especially recommend *The Science of Words* to any serious vocabulary scholar with an interest in all the intricacies of words.

**Vocabulary in the Elementary and Middle School is primarily written for pre-service and in-service teachers who know that words are critical to all that goes on in schools and in life and who have a concern for their students' development and use of vocabulary.** The book is organized into nine chapters: Each brings a somewhat different focal point to the study of words.

Chapter 1 introduces the complexity of vocabulary and answers such questions as "What are words?" "How many words are there?" and "How many words do we know?" Oral language communication is the focus of Chapter 2. It explores how children learn words, the nature of the mental lexicon, and techniques for developing oral language—perhaps the principal means of vocabulary expansion.

Both Chapters 3 and 4 shift from oracy to literacy. Chapter 3 highlights the role of vocabulary as the bedrock component of reading comprehension, contrasting incidental word learning with direct vocabulary instruction and instruction in the strategies of independent word identification. Chapter 4's thrust is toward the need for writers to choose their words with care and precision and to revise what they write. The value of the thesaurus to writers and speakers is also examined. In Chapter 5 the dictionary as a source of word meanings is the primary subject. Four kinds of dictionaries are described (general, bilingual, single-function, and single-topic) and major elements of school dictionaries are presented. Electronic reference works also are discussed.

Chapter 6 is written to put the language pieces, separated in preceding chapters, back together again. Its emphasis is on vocabulary development in interdisciplinary, integrated curriculum projects. Two types of projects are explained: "out-of-the-ordinary" units and community construction projects. Chapter 7 spells out my thoughts about testing word knowledge. Chapter 8 departs from pedagogy and is included to entice the reader with the beauty of words and words used well. In it you will find inscriptions, mottoes, slogans, proverbs, words about words, and more. The final chapter describes and exemplifies seven broad categories of word and language play: onomastics, expressions, figures of speech, word associations, word formation, word shapes and spellings, and word games. In this chapter I stress the value of word play in stimulating and expanding students' interests in language and language learning.

Altogether, Chapters 2 through 9 present explanations, examples, and recommendations for classroom practice in elementary and middle schools. Having been an active teacher and teacher educator for forty years, I am keenly aware that it is the classroom teacher who knows his or her students and their particular capabilities and interests. Therefore, I have not made specific age-appropriate recommendations of the teaching suggestions herein.

It is my hope that readers of this small book will develop their appreciation for the strength, versatility, and necessity of words—words are the foundation on which every theory of language and literacy development must be firmly anchored.

## Acknowledgments

I have drawn upon the work of many people as I prepared this book, and wherever possible, I have credited them directly. Several individuals have been especially helpful to me in the conceptualization and development of this manuscript. I am most grateful to Bonnie Johnson of Louisiana Tech University who served as supportive critic and sage advisor at every step of the way. Alden Moe of Lehigh University has shared his vocabulary knowledge and passion for many years. I have learned much from both of them.

Special thanks to my graduate assistant, James Richard, and my graduate secretary, Tracie Baumann, who have been of immense help in manuscript preparation. Barbara Gates provided cover design ideas that captured the essence of the book. Louisiana Tech University is fortunate to have these sterling individuals within its ranks.

I also want to thank three reviewers who made constructive and valuable suggestions, many of which I have incorporated: Marti Brueggeman of Ashland University in Ohio, Janice K. Davis of the LaDue School District in Missouri, and Eileen Madaus of the Newton, Massachusetts Public Schools. The book is stronger because of their sensible critiques. Finally, I would like to express my appreciation to the people at Allyn and Bacon with whom I have had the good fortune to work: Virginia Lanigan, acquisitions editor; Arnis Burvikovs, acquisitions editor; Marla Feuerstein, production coordinator; and Tara Padykula, copy editor. Their wise advice and editorial talents contributed greatly to the finished product.

# 1

# *Two Million Words and Counting*

*Words are the starting point. Without words, children can't talk about people, places, or things, about actions, relations, or states. Without words, children have no grammatical rules. Without words, there would be no sound structure, no word structure, and no syntax. (Clark, 1993, front matter)*

Words seem like such ordinary things, and most of us take them for granted. We carry on conversations without ever being particularly aware of the words we are speaking and hearing. We rarely stop to think about how we choose the words we use or how we assign meanings to the words we hear. We seem to use words automatically. We get frustrated when a word is on the tips of our tongues but we can't think of it. Where did all these words come from that we recognize and understand so freely? How are we able to process words so readily?

Words are not as simple as they seem. The complexities of vocabulary are an endless source of fascination to language scholars, teachers, poets, and authors. There are many questions about vocabulary that are worth pondering.

What exactly is a word? What does the word *word* really mean?
How many words are there?
Where do words originate?

What is the size and nature of an English speaker's vocabulary?
How are words organized in our minds?
How does a speaker or writer access this inner storehouse of words?
How does our vocabulary continue to grow?

This book is written to introduce you to the absorbing world of words and to familiarize you with what has been learned from research, informed theory, and classroom practices. The first chapter presents some background information about vocabulary and its development. In it I discuss the nature of words, the size of the English lexicon, and the attributes of personal word knowledge. The English lexicon is defined as all the units of meaning in the language whether printed in a comprehensive dictionary or not.

## The Nature of Words

> It comes as a surprise to most people that something as familiar as "word" does not have a simple, straightforward definition. Every native speaker of a language—that is to say, everyone—has an intuitive appreciation of what words are. Reducing those intuitions to precise definitions is not easy, but because the word is such a basic linguistic concept, every serious student of language faces this challenge. (Miller, 1996, pp. 27–28)

Dictionaries vary greatly in how they go about defining the word *word*. Children's dictionaries typically provide very brief definitions such as "a combination of sounds that have meanings" or "labels for meanings." Standard college dictionaries require a long, enumerated paragraph or more and *The New Shorter Oxford English Dictionary* (Brown, 1993, pp. 3716–3717) utilizes four dense, small-font columns of type in its definition of *word*.

The common elements of virtually all definitions of *word* are that words are linguistic units of sound and print that represent meanings and that words can stand alone. In other words, they need not be attached to other units of meaning in the same way that prefixes and suffixes must. There is much more complexity to vocabulary than the oral or written forms that represent meanings.

One confounding aspect of vocabulary is that numerous English words represent more than one meaning. Notice the different meanings of the word *line* in: a fishing line, a line of work, a bus line, a telephone line, the bottom line, the county line, that old line, throw someone a line, drop someone a line, deliver a line, a line of credit, draw the line, and skip a line.

A related but reverse compounding aspect of vocabulary is that many meanings are represented by different words. For example, recall the English words that exist to represent some aspect of intelligence such as *smart, clever, bright, brilliant, quick-witted, sharp, astute, adept, quick, facile, ingenious, apt, erudite, savvy, brainy, egghead.* It is curious that although many common English words have more than one meaning (e.g., *picket line, line of print*) relatively fewer meanings are represented by more than one word (e.g., *smart, bright*). Why does the language have fewer synonyms than multiple-meaning words? No one seems to know.

A third factor that contributes to confusion about what constitutes a word has to do with words derived from other words (e.g., *happy, happiness, happier, happiest, unhappy, unhappiness*). Should each form of a word be considered a separate word? Such derivative words differ in both form and meaning, yet they share a common core of meaning.

McArthur (1996, pp. 1026–1027) differentiates eight different kinds of words. Three of the word types identified by McArthur have particular relevance for teachers.

1. *Lexical words:* These words have describable meanings. They are usually nouns *(cabin, Ruston, breeze),* verbs *(hiked, imagine, standing),* or modifiers *(strong, never, happily).*
2. *Grammatical words:* These are the structure words that serve to link lexical words. Included are conjunctions *(and, because, in case),* determiners *(all, this, many),* interjections *(aha, oops, wow),* particles *(to see, look up),* and pronouns *(they, that, she).*
3. *Onomastic words:* These words are the names of particular persons, places, and things not usually listed in dictionaries but important and often intriguing to children (e.g., Chase Howard, Superior Grille, the Hair Port).

Two additional descriptions of words that need to be noted are the phonological and orthographic form of words. Phonological words are the spoken forms of words and orthographic words are the written or printed forms. Both forms of words need to be addressed by teachers. Initially, on entering school, children know thousands more phonological words than their written (orthographic) forms. The remaining three types of words identified by McArthur, morphological words, lexicographical words, and statistical words are of primary interest to linguists, cognitive psychologists, dictionary writers, and researchers.

Crystal (1995) has articulated a description of the English language lexicon that includes two principal types of "lexemes." In brief, Crystal uses the term *lexeme,* which means lexical unit of meaning, rather than the term *word* because it includes units of meaning that may be longer than an individual word. The lexemes fall into two categories: those that can be generated from morphological rules, and those that are not formed morphologically and whose meanings, therefore, cannot be predicted from a part of the word or expression.

Morphological rules govern the construction of derivations that are noun forms (e.g., *writer, writers*), verb forms (e.g., *write, writes, writing*), derivational suffixes (e.g., *writeable*), compounds (e.g., *ghost writer*), prefixes (e.g., *unwritten*), and irregulars (e.g., *wrote*). The meaning of each derived word is dependent on the base or root word's meaning.

The second type of lexeme includes words whose meanings are not predictable from the rules of morphology. These words are pure units of meaning (e.g., *chipmunk, strange, label*). Such words are morphologically unpredictable; that is, there is nothing within the words that gives a clue to their meaning, therefore, they must be learned through memorization.

Although the term *lexeme* is a more embodying label for the units of meaning in a language, the word *word* is, of course, the common term used by most people. *Word* will be used throughout this book, although at times I will discuss words, idioms, and slang concurrently. Idioms *(to save the day)* and slang *(the Big House)* must be learned in the same ways that individual words are learned because, as stated earlier, their unique meanings are not a composite of the meanings of the individual words within them. Contrast the intended idiomatic meanings with the literal meaning of the words in the following sentences.

| | |
|---|---|
| Has the cat got your tongue? | (Why are you so quiet?) |
| That's a fine kettle of fish. | (Now we've got some problems.) |
| Be on your toes, now. | (Be alert now!) |
| She is down in the dumps. | (She is feeling rather depressed.) |

Idiomatic expressions can be particularly troublesome for students learning English as a second language because the students may assign the idiom literal meanings rather than the intended meanings, and there are great numbers of frequently used idioms in English.

It is apparent that the notion of "vocabulary" is not as simple as it intuitively seems. Some words are generated by rules, but others are not. Words have both an oral and a written representation in English. Some words serve functions of meaning and others, functions of grammar. Many words represent more than one meaning, and some meanings are expressed by more than one word. Some units of meaning are longer than a word but must be learned as though they were single words. Carter (1987) summarized his analysis of linguistic research into vocabulary by noting

> however detailed and systematic accounts of vocabulary will become and however much more refined applications will develop, vocabulary will always be resistant to too great a degree of systematization. Fuzziness is an inherent characteristic of most words when located in context of use. (p. 225)

Where did all these words and longer lexical units of meaning originate? Many English words have been in use for more than one thousand years since the Anglo-Saxon beginnings of English (e.g., *he, her, men, often*). Other words have entered English from different languages. English word origins can be traced to more than 120 languages (B. Johnson, 1999), for example:

| | |
|---|---|
| algebra (Arabic) | opera (Latin) |
| bandage (French) | pizza (Italian) |
| charisma (Greek) | polo (Tibetan) |
| egg (Scandinavian) | sauna (Finnish) |
| frankfurter (German) | tea (Chinese) |
| geyser (Icelandic) | waffle (Dutch) |
| hammock (Haitian) | yoga (Sanskrit) |
| impala (Zulu) | kayak (Inuit) |
| lilac (Persian) | noodle (German) |

H. L. Mencken clarified the importance of borrowing words from other languages:

> A living language is like a man suffering incessantly from small hemorrhages, and what it needs above all else is constant transactions of new blood from other tongues. The day the gates go up, that day it begins to die. (Mencken, cited in Lederer, 1991, p. 229)

Most words have come about through the creation of new words out of old ones using morphological rules for forming derivatives (e.g., *unwind, childlike*) and compounds (e.g., *tugboat*). New words also have been formed through blending (e.g., *television + marathon = telethon*), clipping (e.g., *influenza* becomes *flu*), and forming reduplicatives, which are word repetitions or near-repetitions (e.g., *goody-goody, wishy-washy*). New words continuously enter the language from the technical fields, sciences, and the professions. New abbreviations arise and take on meaning (e.g., *ATM, CD*). New slang expressions appear almost daily (e.g., *buy the farm*), and everyday language usage generates new words (e.g., *edge city, downsize*). We even coin words to take the place of words that are unknown to us or that we temporarily have forgotten (e.g., *thingamabob, doohickey, gizmo, thingamajig, whatchamacallit*).

## The English Lexicon

How many words are there in the English language? This question cannot be answered with any specificity because the number of words changes continually. As many words are added to the lexicon, somewhat fewer drop out of use. Both the Webster and the Oxford dictionaries include more than a half million words (though they include somewhat different listings). Berg

(1993) reported that the *Oxford English Dictionary* contains 290,500 different entry words, but when derivations, compounds, and variant spellings are added, the dictionary presents 616,500 different word forms (p. 4). The English language lexicon is reported to be far larger than that of other languages. According to Denning and Leben (1995), German has fewer than 200,000 words; French about 150,000; and Russian about 130,000 words. Why the differences? That is a question for the historical linguists. Perhaps part of the answer is that there are twice as many native speakers of English (335 million) as that of Russian (168 million), and there are three or four native speakers of English for each single native speaker of French or German (*World Almanac*, 1998, p. 444).

No standard dictionary takes into account the rapidly expanding technical and scientific fields. Nor can any dictionary keep up with ever-changing slang and jargon uses. Lighter's monumental, three-volume *Historical Dictionary of American Slang* contains more than 20,000 entries just in the first volume which was published in 1994. Crystal (1995) estimated that English uses a half million abbreviated forms (e.g., *NATO, FBI*), many with clear lexical meanings. He points out that flora and fauna form an immense lexical pool because, for example, more than one million different insects have been described and labeled (p. 119). Then, add to all of these lists the tens of thousands of English language idioms, catchphrases (e.g., *not a pretty sight*), and proverbs (e.g., *Birds of a feather flock together*), and the immensity of the English lexicon becomes evident. An estimate of two million or more distinct units of meaning in the language—words, idioms, slang expressions, names, scientific labels, abbreviations, and so on—is probably very conservative.

As an example of how continuously new English words are generated, note these slang expressions that entered American English in the 1990s (Dalzell, 1996, pp. 223–226):

| Slang | Meaning |
| --- | --- |
| bump | to relax |
| couch commander | a television remote device |
| blaze, dip | to leave |
| grip | money |
| jag, herb, zeek | a social outcast |
| McJob | a menial, degrading job |
| stoked | completely happy |
| toss chow | to eat |

Words also fall out of use, especially slang expressions. Do you still use any of these terms from the 1970s and 1980s? Did you ever use them (Dalzell, 1996, pp. 168–175)?

| *Slang* | *Meaning* |
|---|---|
| arbitrary | irrelevant |
| beige | dull |
| cheese | something that is outdated |
| dip | to eavesdrop |
| five-finger discount | shoplifting |
| gank | to flirt |
| moldy | embarrassed |
| posse | group of friends |

Not all slang expressions fade out of a language as quickly as some in the previous list. Are you surprised by some of the dates of origin of these slang expressions (B. Johnson, 1999)?

| | |
|---|---|
| clink (1785) | cranky (1812) |
| firebug (1872) | geek (1876) |
| haven't the foggiest (1917) | fleabag (1941) |
| cheapie (1942) | basket case (1952) |

Slang is not the same as crude or profane language. It long has been part of our living English lexicon. Wentworth Dillon's observation about our changing language is apropos:

> Man ever had, and ever will have, leave
> To coin new words well suited to the age.
> Words are like leaves, some wither every year
> And every year a younger race succeeds.
> (cited in Lederer, 1991, p. 216)

Determining the exact size of the English lexicon is, as has been seen, impossible. The English language is comprised of a fluid lexicon of at least two million lexemes, many of which are individual words. What is a certainty is that vocabulary is the one aspect of language that one can never completely master. Nobody knows every word of English, but somebody knows each word. When it comes to words, every person is destined to be a lifelong learner.

## Personal Word Knowledge

A book designed to offer practical approaches to vocabulary teaching, as is the intent of this book, must be based both on what is known about the mental lexicon of individuals as well as what is known about the complexities of words. A valuable scholarly work on our personal word knowledge is *Words in the Mind: An Introduction to the Mental Lexicon* (1994) written by Jean Aitchison, Rupert Murdoch Professor of Language and Communication at the University of Oxford. The mental lexicon is each human's word store, and it contains much more information about each word than can be found in any dictionary. Dictionaries contain definitions, pronunciations, grammatical functions, and sometimes word histories and sample usage—all arranged alphabetically. The mental lexicon contains all that plus visual images, personal experiences, and special knowledge about the words. It is organized not alphabetically but according to sounds and similarities of meanings.

Aitchison discussed the large number of words that humans know and the speed with which we can retrieve words. This large capacity and speed of access indicates a highly organized mental lexicon. The research she reported shows that when listening and reading we can thoroughly search our mental lexicon in less than one second and recognize a real word or reject a nonsense word or an unknown one. We are equally impressively fast at finding the words we need when we produce speech or writing.

In *The Lexicon in Acquisition* (1993), Eve Clark describes research about how children acquire a lexicon. Clark states:

> The lexicon of a language is the stock of established words speakers can draw on when they speak and have recourse to in understanding what they hear. This stock is stored in memory in such a way that speakers can locate the relevant units to use in both speaking and understanding. To do this, of course, speakers have to be able to identify words either by looking them up in memory (for comprehension) or by retrieving them as appropriate forms for conveying specific meanings (for production). (p. 2)

Each of us has a minimum of two mental vocabularies. The first is a phonological vocabulary that we use when listening and talking. We recognize and understand as well as utter each word by its sound. The second, if we are not illiterate, is an orthographic vocabulary that we use to read and write. We recognize, understand, and produce each word by its written form. What else exists within our mental lexicons? It is necessary to consider our receptive or input processes in contrast to our productive or output processes. We receive vocabulary input both through phonological (listening) and orthographic (reading) sources. Similarly, we produce vocabulary output both phonologically (speaking) and orthographically (writing). In other words, we need to conceptualize four vocabularies in our mental lexicon, and if we speak a second or third language, that number multiplies.

Aitchison (1987, Chapter 19) uses the metaphor of viewing each word in the mental lexicon as a two-sided coin. On one side of the coin are the meaning and word class (nouns, verbs), and on the other side of the coin is the sound of the word. These two-sided coins are necessary for the separate functions of comprehension (input) and production (output). Except for a handful of onomatopoeic words (e.g., *splash, buzz*), there is no natural link between the sound and meaning of a word. The German word *hund*, for example, has the same meaning as the English word *dog*. Aitchison asserted that word meanings and grammatical form are organized in semantic fields in the mental lexicon. Semantically related words are organized for easy access when we speak or write.

We link words in our minds semantically in several ways, among them: coordinate words such as *butterfly* and *moth* share similar features (e.g., *they have wings, they fly*); collocations, words that frequently are found together in the language (e.g., *green grass, torrential downpour*); hypernyms, superordinate words labeling a category, and hyponyms, members of that category (e.g., *Flowers: zinnia, dahlia, rose*); synonyms and antonyms, words with similar or opposite meanings (e.g., *shop, store; married, single*).

Word forms also are organized in our minds with similar sounding words (e.g., *hello, bellow, fellow*). This organization helps us recognize and comprehend words that we hear by contrasting them with similar sounding words, hence the metaphor of words as two-sided coins. Aitchison summed this up:

> The mental lexicon, therefore, seems to be a mixed system which has found a workable compromise between the requirements of production and those of comprehension. The component that is required first in each case has imposed its demands on the organization. Production begins with the semantics and syntax, so these are arranged to suit production. Recognition begins with sounds, so these are organized to suit recognition. (p. 224)

The fact that we organize words through a system of semantic similarity has significance for designing vocabulary instruction (e.g., word webbing, classification tasks). The fact that we recognize and store words in memory through their phonological forms has implications for phonics instruction (e.g., pronouncing unfamiliar written words).

How large is our mental lexicon? As is true of every aspect of vocabulary, estimates vary. Clark (1993) reported studies that indicate that children from age 2 on acquire about 10 new words a day, giving them a mental lexicon of about 14,000 words by age 6. In an address to the 1998 conference of the American Association for the Advancement of Science, Lila Gleitman of the University of Pennsylvania reported that children learn roughly one word every 3 days until age 18 months, and then they learn about 10 words a day or 3,500 words a year until age 30. She estimated that most individuals level off at 80,000 to 100,000 words (in press). Graves (1986) conducted a review of studies of vocabulary size completed between 1891 and 1960. His results showed a range for college graduates of 19,000 to 200,000 words. Nagy and Anderson (1984) concluded from their research that 45,000 words are known by high school graduates. Pinker (1994), commenting on the Nagy and Anderson study, observed that those 45,000 words are almost 3 times as many words as the 18,000 Shakespeare used in writing all of his works.

The oral vocabularies of preschool and primary grade children—that is, the words they comprehend and use when speaking—are much larger than their reading and writing vocabularies. Estimates of oral vocabulary size at age 6 vary from 2,500 words (Dolch, 1936), to 14,000 words reported by Clark (1993), and up to 25,000 words (Smith, 1941). Yet most 6-year-olds can read or write very few words, if any. Chall (1987) estimated that it is not until fourth grade that children can recognize in print 3,000 of the words that were in their mental lexicons at age 6. Over time a greater match develops between our phonological and orthographic vocabularies. On the other hand, the receptive word stores (input), oral and written, of most adults remains larger than the pool of words produced in spoken or written discourse (output). At every stage of development we apparently know more words than we actually use. The fact that an individual's vocabulary may increase from 14,000 words at age 6 to 100,000 words as an adult suggests that many more words are learned through active language use than through explicit instruction.

Crystal (1995) reported a small study that was designed to estimate the relative sizes of the receptive and productive vocabularies of adults. Using a procedure in which subjects were shown words systematically selected from a dictionary, the subjects' task was to indicate whether they knew a word well, vaguely, or not at all (receptive vocabulary). They also indicated whether they used the word often, occasionally, or never (productive vocabulary). Crystal found that his adult subjects reported knowing about 25 percent more words than they reported using when speaking or writing. In addressing the problems of estimating the size of anyone's mental lexicon, Crystal observed, "Apart from anything else, there must always be two totals when presenting the size of a person's vocabulary: one reflecting active vocabulary (lexemes actively used in speech or writing) and the other reflecting passive vocabulary (lexemes known but not used)" (p. 123).

A further problem in trying to estimate the size of the average English speaker's vocabulary has to do with the fact, discussed earlier, that thousands of English words have more than one meaning. Linguists differentiate between words that are polysemous and have more than one related sense (e.g., *back the car, back of the garage*) and words that are homonyms (e.g., *bank of the river, a piggy bank*). Homonyms are distinctly different words. The term *multiple-meaning word* will be used to refer to all words with more than one meaning.

Johnson and Moe (1983) found that 72 percent of 9,000 words in common use in elementary schoolbooks had more than one meaning. Some words have many more meanings than just one. The *Oxford English Dictionary* includes 368 meanings of the word *go,* 396 meanings of *run,* and 464 meanings of *set* (Ash, 1995, p. 87). Yet most word counts and estimations of vocabulary treat a word as though it had but one meaning. More than 50 years ago, Rinsland (1945) recognized this problem of multiple-meaning words and their affect on word-count studies when he conducted his classic study of the vocabulary used in students' writing in Grades 1–8. His research team analyzed a total body of 6 million words from student themes, papers, and other writing. Time and money did not enable analyzing the contextual meanings of these words. In other words, *go* counted as one word even if it was used in 40 different ways by the subjects (e.g., *go away, go over your homework, on the go*). Rinsland discovered 25,632 different word forms used, but how many word meanings those 25,632 word forms represented will never be known.

Determining the precise size of the average—or any—English speaker's mental lexicon cannot be accurate or comprehensive. Do we mean the receptive or the productive vocabulary? The phonological or orthographic vocabulary? Which meaning(s) of each word? How do we know if someone actually does know a word? Do different research methodologies give different results? What counts as a word? We probably never will know with any accuracy the size of the average English speaker's vocabulary, but we do know that a child's wellspring of inner language, the mental lexicon, is very large, rich, and complex. Children begin to learn words when in the crib and that learning never stops.

Almost from birth, children have a remarkable fascination with words, and before they ever enter a classroom, they exhibit a natural talent for learning new words. Teachers have the opportunity to build on children's genuine interests and instinctive capabilities as they stimulate and augment vocabulary acquisition throughout the elementary and middle school years. Chapter 2 explores the roles of vocabulary in oral language use and considers how rich oral language activities contribute to the growth of the mental lexicon.

*References*

Aitchison, J. (1994). *Words in the mind: An introduction to the mental lexicon* (2nd ed.). Oxford, UK: Blackwell.
Ash, R. (1995). *The top 10 of everything: 1996.* London: Dorling Kindersley.
Berg, D. L. (1993). *A guide to the Oxford English dictionary.* Oxford, UK: Oxford University Press.
Brown, L. (Ed.). (1993). *The new shorter Oxford English dictionary* (Vols. 1–2). Oxford, UK: Clarendon Press.

Carter, R. (1987). *Vocabulary: Applied linguistic perspectives*. New York: Routledge.

Chall, J. S. (1987). Two vocabularies for reading: Recognition and meaning. In M. G. McKeown & M. E. Curtis (Eds.), *The nature of vocabulary acquisition* (pp. 7–17). Hillsdale, NJ: Erlbaum.

Clark, E. (1993). *The lexicon in acquisition*. Cambridge, UK: Cambridge University Press.

Crystal, D. (1995). *The Cambridge encyclopedia of the English language*. Cambridge, UK: Cambridge University Press.

Dalzell, T. (1996). *Flappers 2 rappers: American youth slang*. Springfield, MA: Merriam-Webster.

Denning, K., & Leben, W. R. (1995). *English vocabulary elements*. Oxford, UK: Oxford University Press.

Dolch, E. W. (1936). How much word knowledge do children bring to grade 1? *Elementary English Review, 13*, 177–183.

Gleitman, L. R. (in press). *Invitation to cognitive science*. Cambridge, MA: MIT Press.

Graves, M. F. (1986). Vocabulary learning and instruction. In E. Rothkopf (Ed.), *Review of research in education* (pp. 49–89). Washington, DC: American Educational Research Association.

Johnson, B. v. H. (1999). *Word works: Exploring language play*. Golden, CO: Fulcrum Publishing.

Johnson, D. D., & Moe, A. J. (1983). *The Ginn word book for teachers: A basic lexicon*. Lexington, MA: Ginn and Company.

Lederer, R. (1991). *The miracle of language*. New York: Pocket Books.

Lighter, J. E. (Ed.). (1994). *Random House historical dictionary of American slang* (Vol. 1). New York: Random House.

McArthur, T. (Ed.). (1996). *The concise Oxford companion to the English language*. Oxford, UK: Oxford University Press.

Miller, G. A. (1996). *The science of words* (2nd ed.). New York: Scientific American Library.

Nagy, W. E., & Anderson, R. C. (1984). How many words are there in printed school English? *Reading Research Quarterly, 19*, 304–330.

Pinker, S. (1994). *The language instinct: How the mind creates language*. New York: HarperPerennial.

Rinsland, H. D. (1945). *A basic vocabulary of elementary school children*. New York: The Macmillan Company.

Smith, M. K. (1941). Measurement of the size of general English vocabulary through the elementary grades and high school. *Genetic Psychological Monographs, 24*, 311–345.

*The world almanac and book of facts*. (1998). Mahwah, NJ: World Almanac Books.

# 2

## *On the Tip of the Tongue*

### *Vocabulary and Oral Language*

*Daily life is conducted in spoken language. Human beings constantly converse, negotiate, discuss, and debate the issues and decisions of their lives; the ability to speak and listen effectively often makes the critical difference between success or failure. (Pinnell & Jaggar, 1991, p. 691)*

Oracy and literacy are inextricably intertwined, but they are not the same. Oracy is the spontaneous process of learning to listen and speak, and literacy is the educational process of learning to read and write. Children learn to speak without being taught; only later do they learn to read and write. Every physically and mentally healthy human being learns how to speak, but a great many humans never master written language. The spoken and written channels are different, and oral language is learned naturally. There are a number of reasons why oral language is acquired more readily than written:

1. Language is oral and humans are born with a natural language instinct.
2. Spoken language has been around for more than 100,000 years. Writing systems are relatively recent inventions dating back only five or six thousand years.
3. Humans are immersed in oral language from the time they are in the cradle.

4. Speech doesn't need to be seen so it works in the dark, or around corners, or over phones, or while doing other things.
5. Oral communication is facilitated by such factors as volume, pitch, stress, speed, modulation, and the nonverbal skills of facial expressions, gestures, eye contact, posture, and personal space. Written language only has punctuation to represent such variables.

We only can marvel at the extraordinary achievement of written language and the enormous intellectual accomplishment of learning to read and write.

Steven Pinker, one of the world's foremost authorities on language and the mind, has described the innate nature of language development.

> Language is not a cultural artifact that we learn the way we learn to tell time or how the federal government works. Instead, it is a distinct piece of the biological makeup of our brains. Language is a complex, specialized skill, which develops in the child spontaneously, without conscious effort of formal instruction, is deployed without awareness of its underlying logic, is qualitatively the same in every individual, and is distinct from more general abilities to process information or behave intelligently. (1994, p. 18)

As early as 1874 in *The Descent of Man,* Charles Darwin stated that humans have "an instinctive tendency to speak, as we see in the babble of our young children; while no child has an instinctive tendency to . . . write" (cited in Pinker, p. 20). Gee (cited in Iseminger, 1998) also has observed that acquiring literacy is more difficult than acquiring oracy, "because reading has no biological underpinnings, as oral language does, and reading is a relatively new twist in human development" (p. 20).

The importance of oral language in vocabulary development has been argued for decades. O'Rourke (1974) observed, "Rich language experiences must come early in the child's development" (p. 48). Nagy and Herman (1987) noted:

> Learning word meanings from oral context is obviously a major mode of vocabulary acquisition, especially in the preschool years. Many, if not most, of the thousands of words that children learn before they enter school are learned without any explicit definition or explanation. (p. 24)

Baumann and Kameenui (1991) stressed the need for longitudinal and developmental research on the impact of oral language context on vocabulary learning and stated, "It would be unwise to underestimate the power of simple oral exposure to vocabulary" (p. 627).

It is clear that teachers could not prevent children from expanding their vocabularies even if they tried. Children, however, come to school with a wide range of advantages or disadvantages. Some have had active participation with parents or caregivers in oral communication, but other children have had mostly passive exposure to the spoken word. Wurman (1992) cited U.S. Department of Education statistics showing that the average kindergarten pupil has watched more than five thousand hours of television, and that is more time than it takes to earn a Bachelor's degree (p. 49). Teachers need to establish learning environments and undertake oral language development activities that will continue the natural vocabulary growth that for many children was dramatic even before they walked through a schoolhouse door. This chapter will set out ways to do that.

## How Children Learn Words

Children begin to learn single words by the time they are a year old, and word-learning goes on throughout life—no wonder, since the English lexicon already contains more than two million words. The window for easy, natural language acquisition, especially syntactic development, seems to begin to close in early adolescence (Lenneberg, 1967; Aitchison, 1997), and there is evidence that in a few bizarre situations in which children were not exposed to language before their teens, the children never learned more than fragments of language (Ingram, 1992, pp. 200–217).

For every child learning any language, three separate but related tasks are required to learn word meanings. The first task is a naming task. Learners must make the discovery that certain sequences of speech sounds that they hear—and later articulate—serve as the names or labels of things. These label words are sometimes referred to as holaphrastic sentences. The sounds heard as "muh-muh" come to be understood as the name "mama," the person who provides love and sustenance. The second task in word-learning requires grouping things that fit together under the same label. Initially the label "doggy" might mean the specific family pet, Bowser, and gradually "doggy" subsumes other specific dogs, breeds of dogs, pictures of dogs, and toy dogs. The third word-learning task involves figuring out how different words relate to one another within and across categories. For example, "doggies" have legs and can run, but "birdies" have wings and can fly. "Doggies" and "birdies" are alike in some ways (e.g., they are pets, they eat), but they are different in other important ways (e.g., fur or feathers, bark or chirp). These three word-learning tasks—naming, classifying, and relating—are significant individual discoveries that begin early in life and are employed in vocabulary acquisition throughout life. Aitchison (1994) calls these tasks labeling, packaging, and network building. She provides thorough descriptions and research support for the three in her chapter "What Is a Bongaloo, Daddy?" (pp. 169–180). Learning to first associate a sound string with its meaning, then learning the related instances of meaning that fit under the same label, and then relating these words to other words in the mental lexicon is quite an achievement.

Learning new words involves both comprehension and production. Understanding what one hears precedes learning to produce the word orally. For both children and adults, the production vocabulary is never as large as the comprehension vocabulary, as discussed in Chapter 1.

The roles of parents, caregivers, siblings, and others in the vocabulary development of preschool children cannot be underestimated. No language or education scholar, of course, would recommend that parents provide their preschoolers with explicit language lessons or repetitive word or grammar drills. Two recent studies, however, support common sense observations that the size of toddlers' vocabularies depends on how much their mothers talk with them. Children require genuine human interaction to attach meanings to words. There is little point in trying to cram vocabulary into the heads of very young children. Engaging in frequent, interactive communication (e.g., conversation and discussion) is the way most preschool children learn most words. The casualness with which children learn to talk, learn to use grammar, and learn new words is a great mystery that can only be attributed to the innate "blueprints" for language, the language instinct, with which all children are born.

Some parents worry about children they think lag behind other children their own age and who seem to be "slow" at learning to talk. Ingram (1992, p. 187) reported an oft-told yarn about a couple and their young son. The tale demonstrates some functions of language that we will examine next and pokes fun at needless parental worries about language delays.

> These parents were becoming more and more uneasy as time passed and their son spoke not one word. There seemed to be no reason why he wasn't talking: he wasn't deaf, and he seemed to be smart enough. But by the time he had reached the age of four and still hadn't spoken, they began to get desperate. One morning when the whole family was seated at breakfast, he shocked them by saying loudly and clearly, "I didn't get strawberries on my cereal." Even in the midst of her delight and relief, his mother had the presence of mind to ask, "Why have you never spoken before?" to which her son replied, clearly annoyed, "Up till now everything has been all right."

Halliday (1969, 1973, 1975) suggests that infants discover that the function of language is to make meanings by encountering and experiencing language for at least seven different purposes:

1. Instrumental function—to satisfy basic needs ("I want . . .")
2. Regulatory function—to influence behavior of others ("Do as I tell you")

3. Heuristic function—to explore and find out about things ("Tell me why")
4. Imaginative function—to explore imaginary worlds ("Let's pretend . . .")
5. Interactional function—to mediate relationships with others ("Me and you")
6. Personal function—to express one's self ("Here I am")
7. Informative function—to communicate information ("I've got something to tell you")

Halliday found that children use language for all seven purposes before entering school. The lad who wanted strawberries on his cereal demonstrated both the instrumental, regulatory, and informative functions of language.

## *The Mental Lexicon*

The mental lexicon contains all the words a person knows. As noted in the last chapter, children may have acquired a vocabulary of 14,000 words by age 6 (Clark, 1993, p. 13). Moe, Hopkins, and Rush (1982) gathered data on the spoken vocabularies of first-grade children and determined that their subjects had oral productive vocabularies of about 6,500 words—fewer than half the words likely to have been in the same children's receptive (comprehension) vocabularies—as would be expected (p. 27). Learners maintain a growth rate of about 3,500 words a year until age 30, for a total vocabulary of close to 100,000 words (Gleitman, 1998). My research has led me to a conservative estimate of 2,000,000 different words in the English lexicon, which means that the average 30-year-old adult knows only about 5 percent of the words that exist. Aitchison (1997) observes, "The only way to begin to account for the child's wizardry as a word learner, given the sheer weight of how much there is to be learned, is that . . . word learning ability is clearly inbuilt in humans" (p. 63). She uses the metaphor of the two-sided coin to describe words in the mental lexicon. One side carries the sound needed for comprehension and the other side carries the meaning and grammatical function needed for production (pp. 62–63).

The mental lexicon of each individual, then, must contain a listing of all the word forms and meanings the speaker knows and a parallel list of the word sounds (and later spellings). The first list is used to produce words for speech (and later writing), and the second is used to receive and interpret oral (and later written) input. The mental lexicon not only contains word knowledge; it also contains *world* knowledge. Word knowledge must of necessity be organized in the mind in such a way for the speaker to know in which contexts a word is appropriate and in which it is not. This "more-than-the-meaning-and-sound" of a word in the mental lexicon holds information of four types, according to Miller (1996, pp. 253–254):

1. *Collocations.* With which word does this word frequently occur in English (e.g., hermetically sealed)?
2. *Syntactic contexts.* The grammar of a language constrains the positions in sentences in which a word can occur and which form of a word can occur (e.g., "Yesterday he took a walk" *not* "Yesterday he will take a walk").
3. *Semantic contexts.* Words must fit with one another according to semantic rules (e.g., The verb *drink* must be followed by a liquid not a solid).
4. *Pragmatic contexts.* These are the world-knowledge contexts in which a word can properly be used (e.g., When inviting dignitaries to a dinner party, one would not ask them to "Come on over and pig out").

The mental lexicon stores all four kinds of contextual information, as well as meaning, form, and sound (and later spelling) for each word known. This is much more information than even the most comprehensive dictionary holds for a word.

One of the most amazing things about the human mind is that it enables speakers to instantly and automatically retrieve words from the mental lexicon needed to carry on communication. It also enables listeners to instantly and automatically understand the words in the stream of speech being heard. Occasionally speakers must pause to reflect when a word is "on the tip of the tongue." Communication is, of course, constrained by the words that have or have not been added to our ever-expanding mental lexicons. Learning and using words is much more than just matching a sound or spelling to a dictionary-type definition.

It would be highly unlikely that any two individuals have identical vocabularies, although people do have many words in common. No one knows all the words of English, but every word is known by someone. A common vocabulary is essential for communication to be possible. A number of word count/word frequency studies have been conducted, and in recent decades computer analyses of large bodies of words have been undertaken. We know that in any word frequency study, the most frequently occurring words (e.g., *the, and, I, you, to, that, it, of,* etc.) are used far more often than other words. In one study the most frequently occurring 100 words accounted for half the occurrences of all 50,000 different words in a body of 1,000,000 words of printed English text (Kucera & Francis, 1967).

Miller (1996) argued the importance of vocabulary development as an essential mission of schooling. He stated:

> A primary goal of formal education should be to ensure that all members of the national community share a common vocabulary—a vocabulary in which

important issues can be clearly phrased, in which questions can be asked and answers debated. Of all the fascinating facts and ideas about words none are of greater practical importance than those pertaining to the growth of a common vocabulary. (p. 255)

E. D. Hirsch, Jr. (1987), in his ground-breaking but controversial best seller *Cultural Literacy: What Every American Needs to Know,* presented a list of more than 5,000 names, concepts, phrases, and dates that he deemed essential for effective national communication. Subsequently he compiled a dictionary of cultural literacy and an eight-book series of instructional texts for elementary and middle schools that would provide the fundamentals of a good education. A new work, *The Encarta World English Dictionary,* released in 1999 and composed of more than 3,000,000 words, was the first dictionary to be derived from a single database of world English.

It is not my intent to recommend teaching a specific set of words to achieve a "national vocabulary" or a "world vocabulary" that enhances communication, although accurate communication is indispensable in any society. I believe that the best way to help schoolchildren expand their vocabularies so that there is a likelihood of ever-improving communication is to provide plentiful, interactive oral language experiences throughout the elementary and middle grades. Such development can sustain and expand on the remarkable achievements in oral language usage and vocabulary acquisition made by children before they ever begin their formal education.

## *Development of Oral Language*

What can teachers do to help children continue the vocabulary growth and language sophistication that has been under way since they were about a year old? Should teachers be concerned at all about oral language development, or should they just get out of the way and let nature take its course? Perhaps that has happened too much because oral language development (oracy) has taken a back seat to reading and writing (literacy) instruction in most classrooms. Olson (1977) found that the longer students are in school, the fewer the opportunities they have to use oral language in the classroom. That may not be true today because many current popular practices, such as literature circles, cooperative learning, buddy reading, and inquiry methods, all include a good deal of conversation.

Pinnell and Jaggar (1991) conducted a comprehensive review of the literature on how children develop their use of oral language. They presented five major and somewhat overlapping implications for teaching (pp. 691–720):

1. Teachers and the curriculum should provide opportunities for children to engage in talking. Children "learn language and how to use it

through social interaction in situations where spoken language serves genuine purposes for them and those around them" (p. 710). These interactions enable children to understand the functions, structures, and contextual rules of language. Through these interactions their vocabularies continue to grow. This implication calls for decreasing the amount of teacher-talk and increasing pupil-talk in the classroom.

2. Students need opportunities to engage in many kinds of talking. "The most effective techniques for promoting oral language development are small-group student discussions and project work, informal conversations between students and their peers and teachers, language games [see Chapter 9 of this book, which deals with word games], storytelling, creative dramatics, role playing, improvisation, and, for older students, more formal drama" (p. 710). Some of these techniques are described later in this chapter.

3. Oral language development should not be left to chance but should be intentional. Deliberate, planned oral communication can serve three purposes: practicing different language functions in specific situations, using oral language as the medium for learning in every subject area (because through talking students construct knowledge), and recognizing that learning any content is primarily learning language.

4. The classroom context and environment are central to oral language use and development in the classroom. In a classroom where the teacher primarily is seen as a transmitter of knowledge whose role is to talk while students listen, the oral language of students will not be enhanced.

5. Oral language is not only a means to gain understanding but is also a way students display their competence. The oral language of students is subtly evaluated by their teachers and their peers.

Last and DeMuth (1991) published a curriculum guide with specific classroom activities in listening and speaking that adopted a functional communication approach. Their guide reflected the belief that organizing oral language development around the dominant functions of language takes into account communication audiences (self, other, small groups, etc.), oral communication media (face-to-face, radio, television, etc.), and communication contexts (family, social, classrooms, etc.). Halliday (1973) identified the seven social functions of language described earlier. Last and DeMuth identified five dominant functions of oral language as a framework for their guide: expressing feelings (affective communication), ritualizing, imagining, informing, and persuading.

1. Affective communication includes language interactions involving expressions of feelings and beliefs. Included are expressing feelings about self ("I feel happy when . . ."), feelings about others ("The thing I

really like about Ms. T is . . ."), opinions ("The school rule I think is most important is . . . because . . ."), and listening empathically ("I can see why . . . upset you so much").

2. Ritualistic communication is taken for granted by most people. Ritualistic functions are real-world processes that include social courtesies, participating in conversations and discussions, and conducting interviews.

3. Imaginative communication includes interactions related to stories, poetry, and drama. Included are learning the rhythms and rhymes used in poetry, role playing characters, and preparing and telling imaginative stories.

4. Informative communication includes giving and receiving information such as directions, descriptions, and explanations.

5. Persuasive communication is used to influence the actions or ideas of others. Included are understanding and applying persuasive strategies in diverse contexts and being aware of such strategies when used by individuals, groups, and the media. (pp. 10–21)

Common threads weave through Halliday's social functions of language and Last and DeMuth's dominant functions of language. These common threads, the social and interactional skills needed to use and develop oral language effectively in context, can be summed up as follows:

1. Conversing and discussing
2. Seeking information
3. Informing
4. Persuading
5. Imagining and telling stories

Learning new words and, thus, increasing the size of the mental lexicon will be a natural by-product of these oral language interactions. They are the very types of interactions through which children rapidly learn language commencing with their earliest preschool years.

## Teaching Suggestions

The remainder of this chapter presents suggested teaching activities for oral language development, which will inevitably result in expanded vocabularies. Although oracy and literacy are not the same, they are acutely and increasingly interrelated as reading and writing skills are learned and perfected. Vocabularies expand and communication abilities grow richer through what is heard and read as well as through the production of spoken and written language. Therefore, some of the following activities rightly and naturally involve aspects of literacy as well as oracy. The teaching suggestions are organized according to the five social and interactional language functions listed on p. 21.

## Conversing and Discussing

Conversing and discussing, called ritualistic communication by Last and DeMuth, encompasses everyday, real-world processes in use when we talk with one another informally or formally. Two activities are recommended:

*1. Conversation Corner.* Most of us engage in conversations every day. It is our most basic form of communication. During conversation we exchange ideas, tidbits of news, feelings, opinions, information, hopes, expectations, and more. Some teachers designate a special place in the room as the "conversation corner" where two or more students may go to engage in quiet conversation or where the teacher can converse with a student or two. Some rules of conversation are established with the entire class. Rules may include bans on gossiping or monopolizing a conversation, and encouraging all to listen attentively when others are speaking. Other rules might encourage participants to ask clarifying questions and stipulations that each member of a conversation group is expected to actively participate. Informal conversation with peers and teachers facilitates development of speaking and listening skills as well as vocabulary growth.

*2. Group Discussion.* Discussion is more formal than conversation and usually has a specific purpose and focuses on a topic. Classroom discussion topics might include a book or story that all have read, a news story or current event, an editorial cartoon that requires inference making, a picture, or a school or class project or event. As with conversation, rules to govern discussion need to be drawn up by the class. In addition to the conversation rules, discussion rules might include the necessity of sticking to the topic, respecting all points of view, attempting to draw one another out in the discussion, and a requirement that discussants state when they are sharing personal viewpoints rather than expressing facts.

Cooperative learning groups typically have two to six members whose purpose is to accomplish a specific task (e.g., plan the construction of a scale-model theme park using mainly recyclable materials), or to discuss a certain topic or component of a topic (e.g., In a unit on the Revolutionary War, different cooperative groups would discuss research and present findings about causes of the Revolution, loyalties to England, the roles played by women, etc.), or to solve a problem (e.g., What are some ways to make new transfer students to the school feel at home?). Cooperative groups have a discussion leader and a scribe as well as contributing members. The more experience students have participating in directed class discussions, the better at it they become.

Panel discussions operate more formally than other types of discussions and are considered one kind of oral presentation to an audience. Each panel has a chairperson who introduces the topic, makes introductions, and guides the discussion. All panel members are expected to make prepared oral contributions. Panel discussions frequently conclude with a give-and-take between the panel members and between the panel and audience.

Daniels (cited in Bromley, 1998) proposed literature circles as a way to facilitate thoughtful reading and student-led discussions. Literature circles are comprised of seven students, each with a different role, who discuss a work of fiction or nonfiction that all members have read. The seven roles and their job descriptions are:

1. Discussion leader who develops questions around the big ideas and feelings.
2. Travel tracer who traces the actions and describes the settings.
3. Vocabulary enricher who finds important words in the text (e.g., unfamiliar or repeated words or unique uses of known words) and clarifies their meanings.
4. Connector who makes connections between the book and real-life people, places, and events.
5. Investigator who finds background information on topics related to the reading.
6. Literary luminary who locates interesting sections of the text to read aloud to the literature circle.
7. Illustrator who draws pictures, diagrams, or other graphics related to the reading. (p. 328)

Literature circles can lead to deepened understandings of a story, help students connect the story to their own lives, and expand their vocabularies through the process of group discussion.

## Seeking Information

Seeking information is the heuristic function of language described by Halliday (1975). It includes the oral processes involved in exploring and finding out about some aspect of the world, including collecting oral histories.

*Oral Histories.* Oral historians are researchers who conduct well-prepared interviews of a person or persons. Interviewees (subjects) are asked about events in which they participated or were observers. Subjects describe experiences, values, and beliefs. Collecting oral histories is not a new endeavor. Ritchie (1995) stated:

It is impossible to pinpoint a place on the globe where people are not now doing oral history. Since the appearance of the first recording devices, from wax cylinder to wire recorder to reel-to-reel, cassette, and videocassette tape, interviewers have questioned politicians and protesters, indigenous peoples and immigrants, artists and artisans, soldiers and civilians, the sacred and the secular. (p. xi)

Establishing an oral history project with elementary and middle school students can lead to valuable outcomes, including the following:

- Collecting oral histories assures a personal involvement in learning.
- Students recognize that each person is a part of history.
- Children who collect oral histories establish relationships with adults and often develop new appreciation and respect for them.
- Pupils realize that all people are important, and every person has a story to tell.
- Students gain experience with many of the social studies disciplines (e.g., history, sociology, economics, psychology).
- Communication skills such as speaking, listening, questioning, note-taking, analyzing information, and forming generalizations are strengthened and vocabulary is expanded. (Johnson & Johnson, 1996, p. 44)

Oral history projects have been undertaken by teachers in every grade from elementary school to graduate school. Students may choose to interview parents, grandparents, other relatives, friends, neighbors, residents of assisted living centers, or others. A general "rule of thumb" is that the subject should be at least twenty years older than the interviewer. Younger children may be advised to focus the interview on only one or two topics such as family and school. Older interviewers may ask about life in "those times," prominent people, current events then, transportation, housing, food, clothing, prices, fads, hobbies, natural occurrences, politics, and more. To begin an oral history project in the early grades, the entire class or smaller groups could do a group interview of an individual; a grandparent, for example.

A class embarking on an oral history project will need to establish some ground rules and interview tips to guide the students. Before the interview, students need to find a person who is willing to be interviewed, select topics, formulate possible questions, and decide whether to take notes or to audio- or videotape the interview. During the interview, students need to be advised to listen without interrupting, to avoid asking questions that can be answered with a "yes" or a "no," to pursue a topic for greater detail, and to avoid sensitive topics such as money or death. After the interview, students need to thank the interviewee and review their notes or tapes while their memories are still fresh. When all interviews have been conducted, the class can engage in an intriguing debriefing discussion during which students can compare what they have learned, share common or diverse impressions, form generalizations, talk about new or unusual words, and other discoveries. The oral history project can be wrapped up by having students prepare "I learned" descriptions of their experiences in the project.

> An oral history project has no losers. Those interviewed have someone to talk with who appreciates their memories. Students doing the interviews benefit in many ways. They learn history—and some of the other social sciences—firsthand. They develop language arts skills, they become aware of patterns of human behavior and language, they get to know someone much better than before, and they come to value that person and that person's experiences. (Johnson & Johnson, 1996, p. 58)

Other classroom interview projects could include interviewing another student, a teacher or administrator, an unforgettable person, someone in another grade, or a person with an interesting occupation or avocation. Actively participating in interviews builds oral language and listening, expands vocabulary, and increases general knowledge and awareness of society.

## Informing

Informing serves the function of giving and receiving information. Presenting information to a group is a form of oral sharing. Sharing begins informally in preschool and kindergarten with "show-and-tell" time during which students tell about an object they have brought to school because they think it might be of interest to the class. Other types of informing activities include reporting on local, national, or world news, giving a demonstration or "how to" presentation (e.g., play an instrument, read a compass, use a thesaurus), describing or "selling" a favorite book or student magazine, or giving a research report. Oral reports can be of a specified time limit, purpose, or organizational format. Teachers model the informing activity before having their students "take the stage." Many students (and adults) are shy and fearful about speaking to an audience of any size. Such students may be more comfortable being part of a group or a panel who share the reporting tasks. Other students love being the center of attention and could talk all day, if permitted.

The success of any informing activity depends equally on the listeners as much as the speaker. When the speaker has something to say and has done some preparation, and when the audience listens attentively, both speaking and listening skills can improve, new words can be learned, and new knowledge and interests can be expanded.

## *Persuading*

Persuading refers to Halliday's regulatory function of language. Its purpose is to influence the behavior or beliefs of others. Two persuading activities are described:

**1. Commercials.**    Advertising is the type of persuasive communication that most of us experience daily. Commercials support what appears on television and radio, and without advertisements many newspapers would be in the red. Creators of commercials use tested devices to sell products and ideas. These devices include sound effects, endorsements by well-known people, and visuals, among others. A major component of nearly all commercials is the spoken or written word (e.g., *hot, new, improved, bright, performs, dazzles, family values, heart, economy, jumbo, giant*). Advertising employs such propaganda devices as:

- Ego building—"People with discerning tastes prefer Stubbies pencils to any other brand."
- Testimonial—"Arthur Shell, Peoria's peanut grower of the year, says, 'The only thing on my bread comes from a jar of PEA-NUT-O spread.'"
- Name calling—"Senator Heavyfoot opposed every motion to provide money for school lunches, but Tom Slick cares about kids."
- Bandwagon—"Get with the crowd. Don't be a loner. Get your Purple Panther sweater vest today."
- Association—"Nine out of ten world-class can collectors subscribe to *Aluminum Gold*, the magazine for collectors. Do you?"
- Children and family—(Using children or family members in the commercial to endorse a product or service, sing ditties, talk in unison, etc.) "My dad will give you the best deal on a new camper. Come see him at Schnabloch's RV."
- Slice-of-life—(An enactment that gives the impression that the commercial is a real-life, everyday experience.) "'Why do you look so grumpy, Marv?' said Marv's wife, Loretta, at breakfast. 'Because this is the third day in a row that we haven't had Toaster Puffs,' replied sour Marv."

Asking elementary and middle school students to log and analyze commercials is an informative experience in learning about persuasive speech. They could design logs that get at the following questions:

What types of products are advertised in the early morning, at dinnertime, during prime time, on Saturday mornings?

Where else are these products advertised?

What new words are used in the commercial?

Which words are used in unexpected ways?

Which words are often repeated?

Which words are alliterative?

How would you classify the commercial (e.g., humorous, slice-of-life, famous person, shouting, before and after, animated cartoon, singing, ego building, etc.)?

After students have had some experience analyzing and classifying commercials and advertisements, have them create and produce their own commercials to present to the class. They may work alone or in small groups. Limit them to a thirty-second commercial, or some students will go on and on. They might invent slogans or jingles, write copy, conduct interviews, give demonstrations, or use any other techniques they observed when doing their commercial analyses. When the commercials have been presented, the debriefing discussion can focus on words used, on clarity, originality, reasonableness, and on what did or did not make a commercial persuasive.

**2. Debates.**    Debates can be formal, highly competitive speech events involving a proposition (e.g., "Resolved: All students in grades K–12 should be required to wear school uniforms"), an affirmative and a negative team with two debaters each, a judge, and a prescribed speaking sequence and format. Middle school, high school, and college debate squads participate in debate contests at local, state, and national levels. It is said that many trial lawyers learned to speak persuasively through participating in school debates.

Debating also can be informal and one of several classroom activities in oral communication. "Mini debates" have the purpose of providing opportunity to speak in front of others and defend views logically. To begin, have the entire class reach a consensus about a topic they would like to debate. The age of your students will help determine the seriousness or sophistication of the topic to be debated. For example:

Students should be allowed to call teachers by their first names.

Anyone old enough to drive a car is old enough to vote.

Providing a nutritious lunch is the responsibility of the school.

All students should be required to tutor a younger person.

No individual or group should be allowed to contribute money to an election.

After the topic has been selected, each student decides whether to speak in favor of it (affirmative) or in opposition to it (negative). The teacher appoints the teams and determines which teams will debate each other. Class time is made available for debate preparation using the library or Internet if necessary. Each debater is to make a two-minute speech in this sequence: 1st affirmative, 1st negative; 2nd affirmative, 2nd negative. Next, teams make comments about the arguments of their opponents and they may ask questions of the opposing team (e.g., "How are you using the word *independent?*"). Finally, one member of each team presents a "persuasive" summary. The debate should last about fifteen minutes. After all teams have debated, a class discussion should lead to consensus about the most compelling arguments supporting or opposing the debate topics.

Debates require active listening, advance preparation of arguments, and persuasive use of research, examples, experience, and common sense—oral communication at its finest.

## *Imagining*

Drama activities help fulfill the imagining function of oral language, and include poetry, stories, and plays, whether orally improvised or developed in writing. Imaginative expression begins in an infant's first year of life with games such as "peek-a-boo" or "making faces." Before their third birthday, children can tell long, detailed, even complicated imaginative stories (Applebee, 1978). Preschoolers frequently engage in imaginative play, and they like to hear, tell, and enact fantasies (Paley, 1987). Elementary and middle school classroom activities that can lead to the development of the imagining function of language include improvisational drama and storytelling, described next.

**1. Improvisational Drama.**   This activity has groups of students working together, and it builds upon the informal "let's pretend" play of early childhood (e.g., playing school, playing hospital). Some improvisational drama is not exclusively imaginative. It may take the form of a reenactment of a real-world event, a piece of children's literature, or a myth, legend, or folktale. Such drama has dialogue but no script, and it differs from pantomime, which uses actions, gestures, and facial expressions but no words. Improvisational drama includes the following steps:

1. Select a story or event to be enacted. The story should include several characters, various actions, and ample opportunities for dialogue.
2. Decide on the characters and who will play them.
3. Plan the sequence of events.
4. Improvise the dialogue.
5. Try out what has been planned.

6. Make revisions of the plans and characterizations.
7. Rehearse again, remembering that dialogue is improvised, not memorized, so it will change a bit in every performance.
8. Prepare simple costumes and props (e.g., a piece of chalk for the teacher, a white apron for the baker).
9. Hold final dress rehearsal with costumes and props.
10. Present the play to an audience of students, teachers, and perhaps parents.

Improvisational drama expands the use of natural language, improves self-confidence in front of a group, and provides enjoyment and many laughs. Other types of imaginative oral language include choral speaking, impromptu skits, readers' theater, and telling stories.

**2. Storytelling.**   Storytelling is an art, and professional storytellers are in demand by schools, libraries, and organizations. Some elementary and middle school teachers develop their own storytelling skills and they inspire their students to become storytellers. A storyteller is not bound by the printed page and therefore can use actions, facial expressions, gestures, and costumes to draw in the audience. A storyteller can use different voices to represent the various characters in the story being told. Some storytellers use finger puppets, flannelboards, or props while telling the story. The benefits of storytelling in schools were summarized by Bromley (1998).

> From kindergarten through elementary school and beyond, children develop their own personal, expressive language when they tell a story. Telling stories stimulates the imagination, inspires creativity, and helps develop a sense of humor. It gives children an opportunity to improvise and compose with language both informally and formally. Storytelling develops vocabulary, heightens comprehension, and fosters social and emotional growth. (p. 337)

Young children can ease into storytelling by beginning with jokes and riddles (wise teachers screen the jokes before they are told to the class). Favorite nursery rhymes, poems, and song lyrics may follow. Wordless picture books require students to tell stories based on the pictures and sequence. Little puppets or a costume may help the shy alleviate their stage fright. After hearing a few good stories told by the teacher and more precocious classmates, other children become ready to jump in and try their hand at storytelling.

Another way to embark on storytelling is to have students share a personal experience (e.g., a day that they were brave, a favorite relative). Nearly every child has a story to tell. Classmates tend to listen attentively because they have had a similar experience or can identify in some other way. Some teachers introduce storytelling through use of a group story. A story starter is told to the class. For example, "When Kip awoke, he didn't recognize any-thing around him. His clothes seemed to have shrunk, and to his great shock, he discovered he had grown a beard. And he was only eight years old!" Students and teacher take turns adding to a story that may likely take off in unexpected directions.

The following steps are recommended by Barchers (1994, p. 109) to cre-ate effective storytellers.

1. Select a story you know well that you think would be of interest to the class.
2. Reread the story several times and list the main points and sequences.
3. Practice telling the story in front of a mirror, and work on refining wording, facial expressions, intonation, and gestures.
4. Plan an introduction that sets the mood and include a prop to draw the audience in.
5. When telling the story, be sure you can be heard, maintain eye contact, and use movement to indicate character changes.

Nearly everyone enjoys listening to a well-told story. But storytelling does more than provide enjoyment with a form of oral communication. It devel-ops poise and a sense of linguistic power that comes from "holding" an au-dience captivated by the story you are telling.

Children come to school with a natural language instinct, highly devel-oped oral communication skills, and a mental lexicon of thousands of words. Yet most children entering school cannot read a word or only very few. Learning to develop one's receptive and productive processes with written language is not nearly as "natural" as learning speech. Learning to read and write has been called the greatest intellectual feat of one's lifetime. The roles of vocabulary in reading and writing are the foci of the next two chapters, as we shift from oracy to literacy.

## *References* _____

Aitchison, J. (1994). *Words in the mind: An introduction to the mental lexicon* (2nd ed.). Ox-ford, UK: Blackwell.

Aitchison, J. (1997). *The language web.* Cambridge, UK: Cambridge University Press.

Applebee, A. N. (1978). *The child's concept of story.* Chicago: University of Chicago Press.

Barchers, S. I. (1994). *Teaching language arts: An integrated approach.* Minneapolis, MN: West Publishing Company.

Baumann, J. F., & Kameenui, E. J. (1991). Research on vocabulary instruction: Ode to Voltaire. In J. Flood, J. M. Jensen. D. Lapp, & J. R. Squire (Eds.), *Handbook of research on teaching the English language arts* (pp. 604–632). New York: Macmillan.

Bromley, K. D. (1998). *Language arts: Exploring connections* (3rd ed.). Boston, MA: Allyn and Bacon.

Brownlee, S. (1998, June 15). Baby talk. *U.S. News & World Report,* 48–55.

Clark, E. (1993). *The lexicon in acquisition.* Cambridge, UK: Cambridge University Press.

Darwin, C. R. (1874). *The descent of man and selection in relation to sex* (2nd ed.). New York: Hurst & Co.

*Encarta world English dictionary.* (1999). Worldwide: Microsoft Corporation, St. Martin's, Bloomsbury Publishing, Pan Macmillan Australia.

Gleitman, L. R. (in press). *Invitation to cognitive science.* Cambridge, MA: MIT Press.

Halliday, M. A. K. (1969). Relevant models of language. *Educational Review, 22,* 26–37.

Halliday, M. A. K. (1973). *Explorations in the functions of language.* London: Edward Arnold.

Halliday, M. A. K. (1975). *Learning how to mean: Explorations in the development of language.* London: Edward Arnold.

Hirsch, E. D., Jr. (1987). *Cultural literacy: What every American needs to know.* New York: Vintage Books.

Ingram, J. (1992). *Talk talk talk: An investigation into the mystery of speech.* Toronto: Penguin Books.

Iseminger, J. (1998, Fall). A truce in the reading wars. *On Wisconsin, 99,* 18–23.

Johnson, D. D., & Johnson, B. v. H. (1996). An oral history project in an integrated reading/language arts/social studies methods class. *The Reading Professor, 18 (2),* 43–59.

Kucera, H., & Francis, W. N. (1967). *Computational analysis of present-day American English.* Providence, RI: Brown University Press.

Last, E., & DeMuth, R. J. (1991). *Classroom activities in listening and speaking.* Madison, WI: Wisconsin Department of Public Instruction.

Lenneberg, E. H. (Ed.). (1967). *Biological foundations of language.* New York: Wiley.

Miller, G. A. (1996). *The science of words* (2nd ed.). New York: Scientific American Library.

Moe, A. J., Hopkins, C. J., & Rush, R. T. (1982). *The vocabulary of first grade children.* Springfield, IL: Charles C. Thomas.

Nagy, W. E., & Herman, P. A. (1987). Breadth and depth of vocabulary knowledge: Implications for acquisition and instruction. In M. G. McKeown & M. E. Curtis (Eds.), *The nature of vocabulary acquisition* (pp. 19–35). Hillsdale, NJ: Lawrence Erlbaum Associates.

Olson, D. (1977). From utterance to text: The bias of language in speech and writing. *Harvard Educational Review, 47,* 257–281.

O'Rourke, J. P. (1974). *Toward a science of vocabulary development.* The Hague: Mouton.

Paley, V. (1987). *Wally's stories: Conversations in the kindergarten.* Cambridge, MA: Harvard University Press.

Pinker, S. (1994). *The language instinct: How the mind creates language.* New York: HarperPerennial.

Pinnell, G. S., & Jaggar, A. M. (1991). Oral language: Speaking and listening in the classroom. In J. Flood, J. Jensen, D. Lapp, & J. R. Squire (Eds.), *Handbook of research on teaching the English language arts* (pp. 691–720). New York: Macmillan.

Ritchie, D. A. (1995). *Doing oral history.* New York: Twayne.

Wurman, R. S. (1992). *Follow the yellow brick road: Learning to give, take, and use instructions.* New York: Bantam Books.

# 3

## *So That's What It Means*

### *Vocabulary and Reading*

*You can't build a vocabulary without reading. You can't make friends if you never meet anybody, but stay at home by yourself all of the time. In the same way, you can't build up a vocabulary if you never meet any new words. And to meet them, you must read. The more you read, the better. A book a week is good, a book every other day is better, a book a day is still better. There is no upper limit. Keep on reading. Keep on meeting unfamiliar words on printed pages. Keep on getting acquainted with the faces of words.* Read. *(Flesch & Lass, 1996, p. 105)*

There are more than 5,000 spoken languages in the world (Altmann, 1997, pp. 231–232). Nonetheless, 95 percent of the world's population speaks fewer than 100 of the languages, the other 5 percent speaks one or another of the remaining languages. On the island of New Guinea alone, 700 different languages are spoken. Twelve of the world's languages are the native languages of at least 50 million people, as shown in Table 3.1.

Spoken language in one form or another has been in use for about 100,000 years, but writing systems are much more recent inventions. Hieroglyphics, a form of writing using pictures of objects to represent words, ideas, and syllables, was in use by Egyptian, Hittite, and Mayan people as long ago as 3,500 B.C. Other early writing systems included cuneiforms and syllabaries. Japanese is a language with a syllabary in which one symbol represents one syllable. Chinese, on the other hand, is a writing system that

**TABLE 3.1**    *The Principal Languages of the World*

| Language | Speakers in millions | | Language | Speakers in millions | |
|---|---|---|---|---|---|
| | *Native* | *Total* | | *Native* | *Total* |
| Mandarin | 863 | 1,025 | Portuguese | 173 | 187 |
| Hindi | 357 | 476 | Russian | 168 | 279 |
| Spanish | 352 | 409 | Japanese | 125 | 126 |
| English | 335 | 497 | German | 99 | 128 |
| Bengali | 200 | 207 | French | 75 | 127 |
| Arabic | 200 | 235 | Malay-Indonesian | 57 | 170 |

*Source:* From *The World Almanac*, 1998, p. 444.

consists of logograms—each character represents a whole word (English also uses some logograms, including $, @, &, %, #, and the numerals). All of the major Chinese dialects (e.g., Mandarin, Cantonese, Wu, Min, Hakka) use a common logogramic writing system.

Modern alphabets, in which one symbol represents a speech sound (phoneme) originated in Syria and Palestine between 2,000–1,500 B.C. The Greek alphabet was devised in about 1,000 B.C., and the Roman alphabet was derived from the Greek in the seventh and sixth century B.C. The Roman (or Latin) script is the basis for the English writing system in use today. Gaur (1984, 1989, 1992, pp. 215–226) presented writing samples, locations, and dates of origin of the 168 most important scripts ever or currently in use—a fascinating display of human creations.

Altmann (1997) stated, "The advent of the written word must surely rank, together with fire and the wheel, as one of mankind's greatest inventions" (p. 160). All written scripts are essentially information storage systems. Writing systems eliminate the need for the personal, prolonged human contact required of oral communication. Once something has been written, the information is available to everyone who has mastered the rules of the writing system. All writing systems belong to one of two groups: thought writing in which the symbols represent meaning directly (e.g., Chinese logograms), or sound writing in which the symbols represent sounds, and the sounds in combination represent meaning. The English alphabet is primarily a sound system in which 26 letters represent, in various ways, the 44 or 45 phonemes of spoken English. Learning to read and write a language is not acquired as naturally as learning to listen and speak; achieving literacy is much more complex than achieving oracy.

## Vocabulary and Literacy

In the last chapter we looked at ways to expand children's vocabularies through oral language activities. Now we must ask, "How do readers learn new words?" There are three general ways in which new words are learned through reading.

Once a child has learned to read, new words are learned from written contexts, even though such contexts are rarely as rich as oral contexts for all the reasons stated at the outset of Chapter 2. Nonetheless, if Clark's (1993) assertions are accurate and individuals maintain a growth rate of 3,500 words a year until age 30, it logically follows that most of those words would have been learned through oral contexts and through reading rather than through direct instruction. One way teachers can increase general, nonfocused vocabulary growth is to have students engage in lots of reading, as Flesch suggested at the start of this chapter.

A second way to help students increase their vocabularies is to teach them skills, generalizations, and strategies that will enable them to learn words on their own. The three types of independent word identification strategies are structural analysis, phonic analysis, and contextual analysis.

*Structural analysis* refers to the morphological clues to meaning that exist in most words longer than a syllable. Prefixes, suffixes, inflections, compounds, acronyms, initialisms all have meanings that contribute to the meaning of the word. The teacher's task is to help children learn to locate meaningful parts of unfamiliar words to get to the words' meanings. Recall that the majority of English words are created from other words through the use of morphological rules (Pinker, 1994, p. 148). These rules give a learner access to thousands of new words.

*Phonic analysis* refers to using letter/sound correspondences to pronounce unfamiliar written words with the expectation that once pronounced, the words will be recognized from the reader's mental lexicon. The teacher's task is to help children learn the letter/sound relations needed to pronounce words they do not recognize in print. The influential publication by the National Research Council, *Preventing Reading Difficulties in Young Children* (Snow, Burns, & Griffin, 1998), reports:

> There is converging research support for the proposition that getting started in reading depends critically on mapping the letters and the spellings of words onto the sounds and speech units that they represent. Failure to master word recognition impedes text comprehension. (p. 321)

*Contextual analysis* refers to using a variety of clues that exist within the context of a sentence or passage (e.g., definitions, exemplifications, synonyms, appositions, descriptions, comparisons) to infer the meanings of unrecognized written words. The teacher's task is to help children learn to recognize and use such clues while they read. Miller (1996) cautioned, though,

> Learning words by reading them in context is effective, but not efficient. Some contexts are uninformative. Some are even misleading. For reading to have any substantial effect on vocabulary, a word must by encountered several times—which means that a great deal of reading must be done. (p. 246)

These three types of word identification strategies (structure, phonics, and context) usually are used in some combination by readers who encounter unfamiliar words during their reading.

In addition to wide reading and applying word identification strategies, a third way in which children learn new words is through direct instruction by the teacher. Direct instruction is called for when a teacher wants students to learn particular words, for example, critical words in a short story, chapter, or article that the class is about to read. Wide reading helps expand a child's general vocabulary, but good, solid instruction is necessary when specific words need to be learned for particular purposes. Later we will examine strategies based on the best of what is known about the nature of instruction and techniques for helping students acquire specific word meanings.

## Semantic Fields

In the 1980s and 1990s, James Burke hosted a series of documentary programs he originated for BBC and PBS television. The series *Connections* was followed by *Connections 2*, created for The Learning Channel. The aim of the two series was to show how inventions and discoveries that may seem to be unrelated are, in fact, connected in surprising ways. The goal of each program was to "invite viewers on journeys that begin in the present day and travel through history to bring to life the extraordinary, associative nature of change" (1994, video jacket). The series captivatingly posed and answered such questions as:

> What has Freud got to do with maps, prison reform, blue dye, disease in the Russian Orthodox church, and the Himalayas?
>
> How are photography, railroads, gaslights, raincoats, blimps, and solar power related to hot-rod driving?
>
> What is the relationship between SWAT teams and hot air ballooning?

*Connections* and *Connections 2* convincingly demonstrated the interconnections and interrelationships of nearly all things.

Connectedness also is true of words. Aitchison (1994) used the term *word webs* to describe the ways in which words are related to one another in the mental lexicon. These semantic networks of interconnected words enable us to select words we want to use as we speak and write. They are part of our internal storage system for the words we acquire through listening and reading. Words are related to one another because they share common semantic elements. The ten types of word associations presented were:

1. *synonyms:* words with nearly the same or quite similar meanings (e.g., *rostrum, pulpit, lectern, speaker's stand*).
2. *antonyms:* words with opposite meanings (e.g., *proud, ashamed*).
3. *collocations:* words that frequently occur together in language usage (e.g., *green grass, unruly behavior*).
4. *coordinates:* words that cluster together on some semantic element but are not superordinate or subordinate to one another (e.g., *Ferris wheel, roller coaster, merry-go-round*).
5. *hypernyms-hyponyms:* A hypernym is the superordinate word in a category (the category label, e.g., *residences*), and hyponyms are the subordinate members of the category (e.g., *apartments, condominiums, houses*).
6. *hypernyms-meronyms:* A hypernym is a whole (e.g., *computer*), and meronyms are its parts (e.g., *keyboard, mouse, chip*).
7. *hypernyms-attributes:* Attributes are the semantic features that describe a hypernym (e.g., *editor: intelligent, well educated, underpaid*).
8. *hypernyms-functions:* Functions are what the hypernym does or what is done to it (e.g., *editor: checks accuracy and clarity, checks spelling, checks style*).
9. *homographs:* Homographs are multiple-meaning words that have the same spellings but different meanings and sometimes different pronunciations (e.g., *bank, ring, record, conduct*).
10. *homophones:* Homophones are words with identical sounds but different spellings and meanings (e.g., *vain-vein, wrapper-rapper*).

Not all words fit neatly into one of these ten categories of associations. Some words belong to more than one category (e.g., *blue* is a color and a mood). Crystal (1995) used the term *semantic fields* to describe the areas of meaning in which words interrelate and help define one another. Words are connected in our mental lexicons in semantic fields. It makes sense, therefore, when teaching words directly, to teach words through their connections rather than through isolated definitions. Ways to do this are presented later in the Teaching Suggestions.

An important "work in progress" related to our understanding of vocabulary is the continuing development of *Wordnet: An Electronic Lexical Database* (Fellbaum, 1998). "*Wordnet* is a semantic dictionary that was designed as a network, partly because representing words and concepts as an interrelated system seems to be consistent with evidence for the way speakers organize their mental lexicons" (p. 7). This electronic database and dictionary browser was designed to "allow users to explore an on-line dictionary on the basis of semantic, rather than alphabetic similarities" (p. xviii). This interdisciplinary, multiuniversity, multiresearch laboratory, government-and-foundation-funded project is working the bugs out of using computational linguistics to process natural language as people do. The basic semantic association in *Wordnet* is synonymy, and sets of synonyms (called *synsets*) form the building blocks.

The most overarching, generic concepts in language have been referred to as "unique beginners" (Miller, 1996, p. 184; 1998, p. 28). Unique beginners can be thought of as "mega-hypernyms." Beneath each unique beginner are all the words related to that concept, be they hyponyms, meronyms, attributes, functions, or other related words. The *Wordnet* (p. 29) project defined a set of 25 unique beginners for nouns under which all of the synsets find their home. They are:

*List of 25 **Unique Beginner Nouns***

| | | |
|---|---|---|
| act, activity | food | possession |
| animal, fauna | group, grouping | process |
| artifact | location | quantity, amount |
| attribute | motivation, motive | relation |
| body | natural object | shape |
| cognition, knowledge | natural phenomenon | state |
| communication | person, human being | substance |
| event, happening | plant, flora | time |
| feeling, emotion | | |

*Wordnet* has organized 80,000 noun word forms related to the 25 unique beginners. *Wordnet* (pp. 70–72) researchers determined that 14 unique beginner verbs would accommodate the more than 11,500 verb synsets in the database. They are:

*List of 14 **Unique Beginner Verbs***

| | |
|---|---|
| motion | consumption |
| perception | creation |
| contract | emotion |
| communication | possession |
| competition | bodily care and functions |
| change | social behavior and interactions |
| cognition | be, resemble, belong, suffice, and auxiliaries |

The two sets of unique beginners, nouns and verbs, could be used in interesting ways to design curriculum materials and instructional strategies intended to help students expand their vocabularies in reading. They could become the central concepts in the word webs described later.

Another vocabulary resource that examined the relations of words within semantic fields was published by Marzano and Marzano in 1988. Based on their analysis of more than 70,000 words commonly found in elementary school texts, the researchers organized words within semantic categories. They used the term *supercluster* in the same way *Wordnet* used the term *unique beginner*. They identified 61 superclusters (e.g., occupations), 430 subordinate clusters (e.g., public servants), and 1,500 subordinate miniclusters (e.g., officers). Within each minicluster they included the words with the closest semantic ties. Some were synonyms, but others were attributes, functions, and so on. The authors recognized the importance of teaching words that are closely related to each other. "Instead of teaching *parch* in isolation, the teacher could introduce *swelter* and *temperate* at the same time, using students' knowledge of one term to help them understand the meaning of others" (p. 24).

Kipfer (1998) has taken the idea of hypernyms and their hyponyms (or superclusters and their clusters, or unique beginners and their underlying components) one step further. Her work was organized around thirteen broad subject areas (e.g., domestic life), and for each subject she presented the hierarchies, structures, orders, classifications, branches, scales, divisions, successions, sequences, and rankings. The author asked:

> We know that orders exist, but have you ever tried to look one up? One can easily enough find the plant and animal kingdoms in the encyclopedias, but how about the organization of the Boy Scouts, the Mafia, or the ranks of sumo wrestlers? No one encyclopedia or other reference contains such a collection of hierarchies and structures in hundreds of different areas. (p. xxiii)

Did you know, for example, that the descending egg size by weight is jumbo (30 oz. per dozen), extra-large (27 oz.), large (24 oz.), medium (21 oz.), small (18 oz.), and pee wee (15 oz.) (p. 312)? *The Order of Things* ought to make a valuable resource for any teacher who wants not only to teach words that cluster together but also to show their hierarchies or divisions.

To summarize the chapter to this point:

- Written language is a relatively recent invention, and learning to read and write is a remarkable accomplishment. Literacy is not acquired as naturally as oracy.
- New words are learned through reading in three ways: frequent reading, learning word identification processes for independent use, and being taught words directly.

- Many words are organized in semantic fields in our mental lexicons to be readily used for communication.
- There are ten principal ways in which words relate to one another.

## Which Words Should Be Taught?

Vocabulary researchers, for at least the past century, have been involved in the development and compilation of word counts and word lists of every imaginable kind. High frequency tabulations include words used in spoken English, children's written English, basal readers, comic books, health education, music, radio programs, safety, World War II, general printed English, and those words deemed essential for leading "the good life" (Dale, Rezick, & Petty, 1973). The most enduring of such word lists was "the combined word list," a list of "sight words" compiled in 1927 by Edmond Dolch. The Dolch list continues to be used by some teachers today.

Should the words on lists based on some type of frequency tabulation be targeted for instruction? I do not think so even though I, too, contributed a word list to the hundreds in existence, immodestly dubbed the "Johnson Basic Sight Vocabulary" (1971). Since my earlier vocabulary work, I have come to realize that most children, adolescents, and adults learn most of the words they know through oral and written communication—through listening and reading, speaking and writing. Does that mean that words should never be taught directly? Absolutely not. Every day in school there are words that must be learned if students are to comprehend what they read and hear, to engage in conversations and discussions, and to write what they know and believe. So the words to teach directly are those the students must learn to be active participants who can comprehend oral and written text.

There is one list of words, however, that I find intriguing. It is a list of one hundred concepts that the linguist Morris Swadesh (cited in Miller, 1996, p. 185) constructed because he believed them to be so basic that every language in the world would have words for them. The list included fifty-four nouns (e.g., *earth, rain, fire, person, water, moon*—but also *louse, grease, horn,* and *liver*). Also included are such high frequency words as *I, you, we, this, that,* the colors, words for size, and so on. Would I make a concerted effort to teach these one hundred words? No, because the important ones will be learned through reading and oral communication, and others, such as *blood* and *kill,* will bombard my students from television often enough.

## Vocabulary Instruction Guidelines

Research and insight presented by such cognitive scientists and language scholars as Clark (1993), Aitchison (1994, 1997), Pinker (1994), Crystal (1995),

Miller (1996), and others referred to in this and earlier chapters have led me to draw up eight guidelines for expanding vocabulary through and for reading.

**Guideline 1.** Word knowledge is critical to comprehension (Davis, 1944). If a reader does not know the words in a text, comprehension will not be possible. Teachers need to devote instructional time to vocabulary growth in ways described in the remainder of this chapter.

**Guideline 2.** Wide reading should be encouraged and facilitated. Thousands of words are learned through reading and oral communication (Nagy & Herman, 1987; Sternberg, 1987). A program designed to encourage and facilitate independent reading is described in the following Teaching Suggestion.

## *Teaching Suggestion*

"Read-a-Million-Minutes." This statewide program was designed to foster wide reading in the state of Iowa. It was begun in 1981 in Denver, Iowa, and has spread to states near (Minnesota, Missouri) and far (Arizona, Georgia) as well as to several foreign countries (Peru, Saudi Arabia). The purpose of the annual month-long endeavor is to encourage children and adolescents to read during and outside the school day. All students set their own personal goals that are totaled for a school goal, which, in turn, contributes to the statewide goal of 60 million minutes. Any reading materials are acceptable—fiction, nonfiction, magazines, newspapers, picture books, comics. An average of 6 to 9 hours (360 to 540 minutes) per student easily has been achieved. This amounts to about 10–15 minutes a night of independent reading.

Each year a committee of teachers selects the theme. In 1996, for example, the theme was "Iowa Roots: Dig In," in celebration of the state's sesquicentennial. Other themes have included tropical rain forests, ice cream, and the solar system. The planning committee prepares a yearly handbook that contains time tabulation forms, sample parent letters, reporting procedures, community involvement activities, activities and games related to the theme for children, bibliographies of teacher and student resource materials, and sample awards and certificates. Students turn in reading time sheets each week that are then tabulated by parent volunteers. School results are sent to the local area education agency for regional tabulation, and those totals are submitted to the state department of education.

Special activities during "Read-a-Million-Minutes" have included pep rallies, sustained silent reading at school and at home, reading to younger children and homebound citizens, weekly assemblies, and special days related to the theme. Many rooms are decorated according to the theme. The "Read-a-Million-Minutes" month ends with a schoolwide, theme-related culminating activity. Activities have ranged from ice cream making, to roller skating, to skydiving exhibitions, to an activity day organized and conducted by education majors from a nearby university.

Students, teachers, and parents alike eagerly anticipate "Read-a-Million-Minutes" month each year. Teachers have reported dramatic increases in interest in reading by their students. Imagine the number of new words learned by the students of a state who read a combined total of sixty million minutes in a month.

**Guideline 3.** Use direct instruction to teach passage-critical words. Passage-critical words are words the teacher deems essential for understanding a text when the text provides insufficient clues to enable the reader to infer the meaning of the words. The report of the National Research Council (Snow, Burns, & Griffin, 1998) reviewed the research and stated simply, "vocabulary instruction does result in measurable increase in students' specific word knowledge" (p. 217). A decade earlier the review of research prepared by the U.S. Department of Education (1997) reported, "When teachers explain exactly what students are expected to learn, and demonstrate the steps needed to accomplish a particular academic task, students learn more" (p. 41). The following Teaching Suggestion explains what it takes to give good instructions.

## Teaching Suggestion

*Direct Instruction.*     Throughout life it is necessary to follow instructions (e.g., how to complete widely different forms, how to assemble numerous products from wagons to coat trees to hose caddies, how to perform functions, how to behave in various situations, how to vote, etc.). But where are the instructions for how to *follow* instructions or how to *create* and *give* instructions? In today's schools, we emphasize useful content, processes, skills, and values, but we seemingly do not teach how to give and receive instructions. One of the most informative books I have encountered about the nature of instruction is *Follow the Yellow Brick Road: Learning to Give, Take, and Use Instructions* (Wurman, 1992). Wurman noted, "Instructions are one of the most *fundamental* aspects of human life. Instructions are the driving force of communications; either explicitly or implicitly, they motivate us to communicate" (p. 11). He also stated that without instructions, most information is useless.

Five elements of instructions (pp. 17–18) should be considered by teachers as they prepare to teach children new words—or anything else.

1. The givers who originate the instruction (teachers)
2. The takers who act on the instruction (students)
3. The content of the instruction (message)
4. The channel or medium of the instruction (oral/written, words/pictures, etc.)
5. The context or setting in which the instruction is to be delivered (classroom, take-home, etc.)

Wurman recommended that the person creating the instruction (the teacher) needs to incorporate six building blocks into the content of the instruction. The building blocks include the mission (purpose), destination (objective), core (procedure), time, anticipation, and failure. Definitions and examples of the building blocks are:

*Mission.*   The general, intangible aim of the instruction, or what the teacher hopes to accomplish. (For example, to teach fifteen words critical to understanding the upcoming social studies chapter so that the chapter will be understood.)

*Destination.*   The tangible, observable end result of the instruction. The point of culmination. (For example, students will be able to provide a synonym, antonym, or otherwise associated word for each of the fifteen words and will be able to create an appropriate context for each word. Ultimately, the students will be able to read and comprehend the social studies chapter.)

*Core.*   The heart of the instruction, the actual directions. (For example, present the fifteen words in two ways. Embed each target word in a list of four synonyms, antonyms, collocations, or coordinates. Discuss with the students how the target word is alike or different from the other words in its list. Then present each target word in an actual sentence or two excerpted from the social studies chapter. Have students create for each word a new context that would make sense.)

*Time.*   The estimated time it will take the teacher and the student. (For example, it will take the teacher twenty-five minutes to introduce the target words and lead a discussion of them. It will take an additional twenty minutes for the students to use the target words in new contexts.)

*Anticipation.*   This is what hurdles the student can expect to encounter along the way. (For example, "You may find it easier to come up with a synonym for the new word than to place it in a new sentence you write. Don't worry, the ability to create context will improve with practice.")

*Failure.*   These are the points or signs that would indicate to the student failure to follow instructions (for example, "When you read the chapter, if you still have trouble understanding any of the fifteen new words, let me know so I can help you.") (Wurman, pp. 163–175).

An important part of teaching—right up there with enthusiasm, high expectations, subject matter knowledge, and respect for students—is clarity of presentation. Students must understand the instructions and know what they are expected to do. Wurman's suggestions for creating clear, understandable instructions should be helpful to teachers as they prepare lessons. For decades teachers have heard about the teach-practice-apply transfer model. Wurman's guidelines help flesh out what needs to be considered to fulfill the model.

**Guideline 4.**  Learning new words requires active involvement with the word—not passive learning of dictionary definitions (Stahl, 1986).

## Teaching Suggestions

*1. Active Involvement with Words.*   "Vocabulary teaching methods which gave only definitional information about each word's meaning did not appear to significantly improve comprehension," was the finding of Stahl (1986, p. 665), based on his meta-analysis of fifty-two vocabulary instruction studies. Active involvement with words takes many different forms in the classroom, including playing word games such as those described in Chapter 9, discussing words in literature circles such as the one discussed in Chapter 2, and participating in the creation of word webs along the lines of those described next. Additionally, using new words in writing and speech, creating drawings of words, doing word searches on the Internet, finding semantically related words in a thesaurus, using the words in skits, creating song lyrics, and making personal word banks are alternatives to passive encounters with words (i.e., looking them up in a dictionary). Simply discussing new words with classmates and then "trying them out" at home can be helpful.

*2. Word Webs.*   Word webs are graphic organizers that present related words and show the nature of the relationships between the words and a central concept. Word webs have been described and labeled in different ways (e.g., "semantic maps," Johnson & Pearson, 1978, 1984; "webs," Marzano & Marzano, 1988; "semantic webs," "word maps," "clusters," etc.). The term *word web* reflects the organization of words in the mental lexicon. Words on the web may relate to the central concept in many ways. They may be synonyms, antonyms, hyponyms (subordinate words), meronyms (parts of a whole), attributes, functions, homographs, homophones, examples, or others. Figure 3.1 shows a word web built around the concept *comic.*

**FIGURE 3.1** *Word Web for* comic

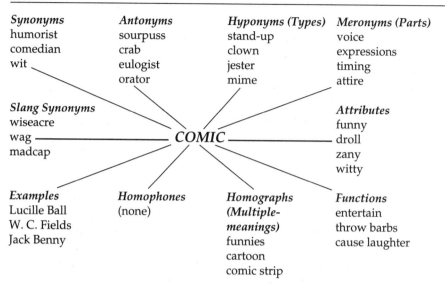

| *Synonyms* | *Antonyms* | *Hyponyms (Types)* | *Meronyms (Parts)* |
| --- | --- | --- | --- |
| humorist | sourpuss | stand-up | voice |
| comedian | crab | clown | expressions |
| wit | eulogist | jester | timing |
| | orator | mime | attire |

*Slang Synonyms*
wiseacre
wag
madcap

**COMIC**

*Attributes*
funny
droll
zany
witty

| *Examples* | *Homophones* | *Homographs* | *Functions* |
| --- | --- | --- | --- |
| Lucille Ball | (none) | *(Multiple-* | entertain |
| W. C. Fields | | *meanings)* | throw barbs |
| Jack Benny | | funnies | cause laughter |
| | | cartoon | |
| | | comic strip | |

Creating word webs is a group or whole-class, not independent, activity because discussing the words on the web and using them in appropriate contexts are critical to the success of the activity (Stahl & Vancil, 1986). Teachers who use word web strategies typically follow steps similar to these:

1. Place the central concept on the chalkboard (e.g., *comic*). Central concepts could be the topic of a chapter to be read, a seasonal theme, or even one of the twenty-five noun and fourteen verb "unique beginners" listed earlier in this chapter.
2. List two or three categories related to the central concept (e.g., synonyms, types, attributes).
3. Choose one of the categories and list two or three members of that category (e.g., attributes: *funny, droll, zany*).
4. Introduce the students to this "starter web" and have them independently add words and categories to a web they prepare at their own desks. Allow students plenty of time to reflect and to activate their prior knowledge. Reflection enables even the slowest learners to think of words to contribute to the class word web.
5. Have students recommend words and categories to add to the growing word web on the chalkboard. Students should expand their own webs by adding the contributions of their classmates.
6. Discussion is the key to word webbing. Lead your students in a discussion of how the words are alike and different. Discuss semantic

subtleties. Have children try out new words in various oral and written contexts.

Several researchers have demonstrated the effectiveness of webbing in helping students learn new words and comprehend related text. The procedure is theoretically sound (Clark, 1993; Aitchison, 1994; Miller, 1996) and experimentally valid (Johnson, Toms-Bronowski, & Pittelman, 1983; Jones, 1984; Karbon, 1984). Word webbing helps students learn new words in a manner that mirrors how words are stored in the mental lexicon. An added benefit is that webbing is not expensive. All the teacher needs is a piece of chalk and some time.

In addition to its use with vocabulary development, webbing is used to help students access their prior knowledge before reading a selection, to serve as the prewriting step of the writing process, and as a form of outlining and note taking less daunting than the traditional procedures. The International Reading Association has published a helpful little work that gives teaching suggestions for word webbing: *Semantic Mapping: Classroom Applications* (Heimlich & Pittelman, 1986).

**Guideline 5.**   Readers must have repeated exposures to a word to learn it well (Miller, 1996). To know a word means knowing what it means, how it fits with related words, how to pronounce it and write it, and the contexts in which it can occur. Repeated exposures to a word ideally should be of three types: concept associations with related words (e.g., synonyms, antonyms, hyponyms, etc.), contextual usage with examples of appropriate contexts, and definition validation.

## Teaching Suggestion

*Multiple Exposures.*   The words that are critical to comprehending a selection frequently are not directly related to one another. Time will not permit creating a separate word web for each passage-critical word. Learning unrelated but critical words can be enhanced when each of the words is presented in three ways: through semantic associations, through context, and through definitions. Note the following sample minilesson:

*Target Words:*   *fliers, phony, alarm*

*Context Activity:*   Students predict the meanings of the target words and discuss their predictions in class. They should not be asked to write definitions for the words (see vocabulary Guideline 6).

"I am no *phony*. I'd never lie to you."

"Tucker has a job handing out *fliers* for Casey's. Business hasn't been so good."

"Instead of looking relaxed, Juanita's face showed *alarm*."

*Semantic Association Activity:*   Students are to add one of the target words to the other words in a category.

| *Ways to Advertise* | *Words for* Fear | *Opposites of* Sincere |
| --- | --- | --- |
| billboards | fright | fake |
| television spots | dread | fraud |
| (fliers) | (alarm) | (phony) |

Next, have the students discuss how the words in each category are alike and different and what some appropriate contexts for the words might be (e.g., to feel *fright* in a scary movie, to feel *dread* when we learn a loved one has been in a terrible accident, to feel *alarm* when hearing footsteps behind you on a deserted street at night).

*Definition Activity:*   Once students have experienced the words contextually and through semantic associations, they are ready to examine a dictionary-type definition of each word. You may want to have them match a word with its definition:

a sheet of paper advertising something or someplace *(flier)*
fake *(phony)*
terror *(alarm)*

Providing students with repeated exposures such as these has been shown to be effective (Stahl, 1986). Such teaching, however, can eat up a great deal of time. You may want to reserve such intensive instruction for those words you feel your students must know.

**Guideline 6.**   Requiring students to write definitions of words is not recommended. Miller (1996) observes, "composing good constructive definitions is an art . . . without special training, most people have trouble defining words whose meanings they know perfectly well" (p. 249). Aitchison (1997) also noted, "Humans cannot usually explain the meanings of the tens of thousands of words they use. Defining words like a dictionary is a technical skill which mostly only lexicographers acquire" (p. 64). Sensible ways to make use of dictionaries are described in Chapter 5.

**Guideline 7.** Successful vocabulary strategies help students relate new words to their own prior knowledge, as well as to other related words. "Children learn vocabulary better when the words they study are related to familiar experiences and to knowledge they already possess. . . . Encouraging students to talk about personal experiences associated with particular words helps them grasp meanings and relationships among new words. . . ." (*What Works*, 1987, p. 33).

**Guideline 8.** Students need to develop strategies for acquiring new words independently from written and oral contexts (Johnson & Baumann, 1984). Independent strategies fall into three broad categories: phonic analysis, structural analysis, and contextual analysis. They are described in the following Teaching Suggestions.

## Teaching Suggestions

*1. Phonic Analysis.* The purpose of phonics is to help readers pronounce words they do not recognize in print. The assumption is that once the unfamiliar printed word is pronounced and they hear its sound, it will become meaningful because it already exists in the child's mental lexicon. (Remember, the typical 6-year-old has about 14,000 words in the mental lexicon, but most can read only a few.) Aitchison's metaphor of words as two-sided coins is relevant here. One side of the coin is the word's sound. It is the sound of the word that enables the reader to relate it to a known word meaning in the mental lexicon (1994, chap. 19). Phonics instruction encompasses a number of teaching and practice methods to help a child learn the hundreds of relationships that exist between the 26 letters and 44 or 45 phonemes of English. Learning these relationships is what helps young readers pronounce the words to hear them and get at their meanings. Phonics does nothing more. It can't teach anyone new words, only those whose meanings they already know. But that is quite enough. In English, writing represents sound and sound represents meaning. Readers interested in learning a variety of specific techniques for teaching children phonics are referred to recent books by Cunningham (1995), McGuinness (1997), Heilman (1998), Ericson and Juliebo (1998), Hull and Fox (1998), and Eldredge (1999).

*2. Structural Analysis.* The purpose of structural analysis is to help readers determine the meanings of unfamiliar printed words by noting the morphemes (i.e., meaningful parts) within the words. Most English words were created through use of morphological rules (e.g., word building rules related to adding prefixes, derivational and inflectional suffixes to root words; compounding; contracting; abbreviating; etc.). Thus, most English words contain clues to their meanings within the word structure. For information about morphological (structural) elements of English and teaching ideas related to them, I refer you to the works of Horowitz (1971), O'Rourke (1974), and Denning and Leben (1995).

**3. Contextual Analysis.** The purpose of contextual analysis is to help readers infer the meanings of unfamiliar words through noting meaningful clues within the context of the sentence or paragraph (Sternberg, 1987, pp. 91–92). Descriptions of different types of context clues and complete discussions of learning words from context can be found in O'Rourke (1974); Nagy, Herman, and Anderson (1985); and Drum and Konopak (1987).

Readers rarely rely on only one of the three processes to identify unfamiliar words. A reader bumping into a new word automatically tries to pronounce it, vocally or subvocally, looks for meaningful parts, and checks a tentative meaning against the sense of the context.

It is apparent that vocabulary is a crucial element in comprehension. If we do not know the words, we cannot understand what we read. Happily, the more we read, the larger our vocabularies are likely to become. Words are as essential to the writing process as they are to reading, and that is the subject of the next chapter, "Just the Right Word: Vocabulary and Writing."

*References*

Aitchison, J. (1994). *Words in the mind: An introduction to the mental lexicon* (2nd ed.). Oxford, UK: Blackwell.

Aitchison, J. (1997). *The language web.* Cambridge, UK: Cambridge University Press.

Altmann, G. T. M. (1997). *The ascent of Babel: An exploration of language, mind, and understanding.* Oxford, UK: Oxford University Press.

Burke, J. (1994). *Connections 2.* New York: Ambrose Video Publishing, Inc.

Clark, E. (1993). *The lexicon in acquisition.* Cambridge, UK: Cambridge University Press.

Cobley, P., & Jansz, L. (1997). *Introducing semiotics.* New York: Totem Books.

Crystal, D. (1995). *The Cambridge encyclopedia of the English language.* Cambridge, UK: Cambridge University Press.

Cunningham, P. M. (1995). *Phonics they use: Words for reading and writing* (2nd ed.). New York: HarperCollins.

Dale, E., Rezik, T., & Petty, W. (1973). *Bibliography of vocabulary studies* (3rd ed.). Columbus, OH: The Ohio State University.

Davis, F. (1994). Fundamental factors of comprehension in reading. *Psychometrika, 9,* 185–197.

Denning, K., & Leben, W. R. (1995). *English vocabulary elements.* Oxford, UK: Oxford University Press.

Dolch, E. (1927). Grade vocabularies. *Journal of Educational Research, 16,* 16–26.

Drum, P. A., & Konopak, B. C. (1987). Learning word meanings from written context. In M. G. McKeown & M. E. Curtis (Eds.), *The nature of vocabulary acquisition* (pp. 73–87). Hillsdale, NJ: Lawrence Erlbaum Associates.

Eldredge, J. L. (1999). *Phonics for teachers: Self-instruction, methods, and activities*. Columbus, OH: Merrill.

Ericson, L., & Juliebo, M. F. (1998). *The phonological awareness handbook for kindergarten and primary teachers*. Newark, DE: International Reading Association.

Fellbaum, C. (Ed.). (1998). *Wordnet: An electronic lexical database*. Cambridge, MA: The MIT Press.

Flesch, R., & Lass, A. H. (1996). *The classic guide to better writing*. New York: HarperPerennial.

Gaur, A. (1984, 1989, 1992). *A history of writing*. New York: Cross River Press.

Heilman, A. W. (1998). *Phonics in proper perspective* (8th ed.). Columbus, OH: Merrill.

Heimlich, J., & Pittelman, S. (1986). *Semantic mapping: Classroom applications*. Newark, DE: International Reading Association.

Horowitz, E. (1977). *Words come in families*. New York: Hart Publishing Company.

Hull, M. A., & Fox, B. J. (1998). *Phonics for the teacher of reading* (7th ed.). Columbus, OH: Merrill.

Johnson, D. D. (1971). A basic vocabulary for beginning reading. *Elementary School Journal, 72* (1), 29–34.

Johnson, D. D., & Baumann, J. F. (1984). Word identification. In P. D. Pearson (Ed.), *Handbook of research in reading* (pp. 583–608). New York: Longman.

Johnson, D. D., & Pearson, P. D. (1978). *Teaching reading vocabulary*. New York: Holt, Rinehart and Winston.

Johnson, D. D., & Pearson, P. D. (1984). *Teaching reading vocabulary* (2nd ed.). Fort Worth, TX: Holt, Rinehart and Winston.

Johnson, D. D., Toms-Bronowski, S., & Pittelman, S. (1982). *An investigation of the effectiveness of semantic mapping and semantic feature analysis with intermediate grade level children* (Program Report 83-3). Madison, WI: Wisconsin Center for Education Research, University of Wisconsin.

Jones, S. T. (1984). *The effects of semantic mapping on vocabulary acquisition and reading comprehension of inner city Black students*. Unpublished doctoral dissertation, University of Wisconsin, Madison.

Karbon, J. C. (1984). *An investigation of the relationships between prior knowledge and vocabulary development using semantic mapping with culturally diverse students*. Unpublished doctoral dissertation, University of Wisconsin, Madison.

Kipfer, B. A. (1997, 1998). *The order of things: How everything in the world is organized into hierarchies, structures, and pecking orders*. New York: Random House.

Marzano, R. J., & Marzano, J. S. (1988). *A cluster approach to elementary vocabulary instruction*. Newark, DE: International Reading Association.

McGuinness, D. (1997). *Why our children can't read: And what we can do about it*. New York: The Free Press.

Miller, G. A. (1996). *The science of words* (2nd ed.). New York: Scientific American Library.

Miller, G. A. (1998). Nouns in Wordnet. In C. Fellbaum (Ed.), *Wordnet: An electronic lexical database* (pp. 23–46). Cambridge, MA: The MIT Press.

Nagy, W. E., & Herman, P. A. (1987). Breadth and depth of vocabulary knowledge: Implications for acquisition and instruction. In M. G. McKeown & M. E. Curtis (Eds.), *The nature of vocabulary acquisition* (pp. 19–35). Hillsdale, NJ: Lawrence Erlbaum Associates.

Nagy, W. E., Herman, P. A., & Anderson, R. C. (1985). Learning words from context. *Reading Research Quarterly, 20,* 233-253.

O'Rourke, J. P. (1974). *Toward a science of vocabulary development*. The Hague: Mouton.

Pinker, S. (1994). *The language instinct: How the mind creates language*. New York: HarperPerennial.

Snow, C. E., Burns, M. S., & Griffin, P. (Eds.). (1998). *Preventing reading difficulties in young children*. Washington, D.C.: National Academy Press.

Stahl, S. (1986). Three principles of effective vocabulary instruction. *Journal of Reading, 29* (7), 662–668.

Stahl, S., & Vancil, S. (1986). Discussion is what makes semantic maps work in vocabulary instruction. *The Reading Teacher, 40,* 62–69.

Sternberg, R. J. (1987). Most vocabulary is learned from context. In M. G. McKeown & M. E. Curtis (Eds.), *The nature of vocabulary acquisition* (pp. 89–105). Hillsdale, NJ: Lawrence Erlbaum Associates.

U.S. Department of Education. (1987). *What works: Research about teaching and learning* (2nd ed.). Washington, D.C.: Author.

*The world almanac and book of facts.* (1998). Mahwah, NJ: World Almanac Books.

Wurman, R. S. (1992). *Follow the yellow brick road: Learning to give, take, & use instructions*. New York: Bantam Books.

# 4

## *Just the Right Word*

### *Vocabulary and Writing**

*Writers love words. And while some writers get excited over a particular pen or a more powerful word processing program, words remain the most important tool the writer has to work with . . . a rich vocabulary allows a writer to get a richness of thought onto the paper. However, the writer's real pleasure comes not from using an exotic word but from using the right word. (Fletcher, 1993)*

Words serve different purposes when we read and when we write. A reader needs to recognize words and assign meanings to them; a writer must choose words to convey ideas. The reader decodes words into meanings, but the writer encodes ideas into words. Readers often get the sense of a word from the narrow or broad context in which it is found. Writers have the obligation to be more precise and must use the right word that best transmits the intended sense. The communication process is successful to the degree that the reader can approximate the same ideas the writer had in mind. It is not the words themselves that are so critical. Rather it is the rich reservoir of meaning underlying the words that counts. Words simply are summary symbols for concepts, labels that facilitate the communication of meanings.

---

*Portions of this chapter appeared in a chapter by the same name and the same author in *Perspectives on Writing: Research, Theory, and Practice* (2000).

Poets, songwriters, novelists, and journalists always have been fascinated with words. Since the late 1800s, teachers, education researchers, textbook publishers, and psychologists also have displayed an interest in vocabulary study. Some of the great names in language research are persons who have undertaken large-scale studies designed to generate word lists. The names Edward Thorndike, Ernest Horn, Henry Rinsland, and Edgar Dale are well known to any student of language and literacy research.

Thorndike analyzed a body of words found in general reading materials and ranked them on frequency of occurrence. This research led to the publication of the acclaimed *The Teacher's Word Book of 20,000 Words* (1931). A later study with Lorge was published as *The Teacher's Word Book of 30,000 Words* (1944). Thorndike's work was the standard vocabulary corpus until the publication of Kucera and Francis's computer analysis in 1967. An oft-cited study of the speaking vocabulary of primary-grade children was published by Murphy in 1957. It continued to be a benchmark of oral vocabulary until the publication of the computer analysis of 200,000 words of oral language used by first-graders conducted by Moe, Hopkins, and Rush in 1982.

Of greater pertinence to the present chapter are three studies that created word lists from the written language of children and adults. Horn (1926) completed an analysis of the words adults use in their writing, primarily letters, and published *A Basic Writing Vocabulary: 10,000 Words Most Commonly Used in Writing*. Rinsland's (1945) *A Basic Vocabulary of Elementary School Children* made a lasting contribution, and it will be described in detail next. Hillerich's *A Writing Vocabulary of Elementary Children* (1978) is an analysis of a smaller corpus of words than Rinsland examined, but it presents more current data. In the studies cited earlier, Thorndike and Lorge's corpus was four and one-half million words, Horn's total was five million, and Rinsland's was six million. Hillerich's word count was about four hundred thousand words.

Rinsland was the first researcher to broadly sample the writings of children in all elementary grades from across the United States. His study was begun in 1936 under a grant from the Works Projects Administration of Oklahoma. The study was designed to do what no other vocabulary research previously had done:

1. to broadly sample children's writing,
2. to gather continuous data for all eight grades,
3. to provide raw frequencies for each word in each grade,
4. to provide a ranked listing based on frequency, and
5. to provide a comparable measure of frequencies across grades.

Rinsland's ultimate goal was to generate a scientifically determined basic vocabulary list that would be useful to the writers of schoolbooks. Rinsland contacted the administrators of fifteen hundred schools within all the geographic, economic, and social strata of the country, requesting original and genuine materials written by children. The project and its value were described.

He asked that the writings include personal notes, stories, poems, compositions, exam papers, reports, and observations. A total of 708 schools (47 percent) responded. "Each paper was read by a number of experienced teachers familiar with children's work in the respective grades to determine authenticity or naturalness of the children's compositions" (1945, p. 7). To ensure uniformity of treatment, 9 rules for tabulation were established. Rinsland followed the Horn model wherein plurals, contractions, and other inflections, derivations, and abbreviations were each treated as a separate word because "children experience some difficulty in learning derivatives" (p. 8) and because "this list is to be used for teaching children" (p. 8). This practice by Rinsland tended to enlarge the total count. Another of Rinsland's tabulation rules, however, must have greatly reduced the size of the count. "Delete slang, provincialisms, colloquial expressions, as determined by the dictionary, as well as trade names and proper names of persons and places, except very well-known terms" (p. 8). Tabulators also were instructed to delete "baby talk." All 6,012,359 words in the corpus were hand tabulated, recorded on large sheets of paper, entered in ledgers, and checked. The reader is reminded that studies such as the Rinsland, Horn, and Thorndike works were undertaken before computers were available to facilitate data reduction. Recall that Rinsland's study was begun in 1936 and the final report was published in 1945.

The Rinsland team found 25,632 different words from the total sample of 6,012,359 words. Different words ranged from 5,099 in Grade 1 to 17,930 in Grade 8. Total words written ranged from 353,874 in Grade 1 to 1,088,343 in Grade 8 (p. 12). Older students obviously wrote more and used a greater quantity of different words than did younger students. As mentioned earlier, Rinsland discovered early in the tabulation process that a serious problem existed because English has so many multiple-meaning words. This problem has existed with nearly all word-count studies. Textbook writers, teachers, and others who were interested in using words found in the productive writing vocabularies of schoolchildren, however, have realized the value of the compilation of words prepared by Rinsland.

## Vocabulary and Writing

Writers with a purpose recognize the importance of words. In an article titled, "Dear Mrs. Roosevelt: Cries for Help from Depression Youth" (*Social Education*, 1996, pp. 271–276), Robert Cohen included letters written to First

Lady Eleanor Roosevelt during the depths of the Great Depression. The following excerpt was the opening of a letter written by a thirteen-year-old Arkansas girl in the winter of 1936.

> I am writing you for some of your old soiled dresses if you have any. I am a poor girl who has to stay out of school on account of dresses, and slips, and a coat. I am in the seventh grade in school but I have to stay out of school because I have not books or clothes to ware. I am in need of dresses and slips and a coat very bad. (p. 272)

An eleventh-grader in Georgia wrote:

> I wish to have my teeth attended to. I'm having a terrible time with two of my teeth. . . . My mouth gets sore and it hurts all the time. All my teeth are decayed except my front teeth and they are starting to decay. I can't have them fixed because my daddy hasn't the money to fix them and he only says teeth are supposed to come out sometime but this is all the teeth I'll ever have. I've shedded all the teeth I'm supposed to. (p. 272)

These letters are as powerful as they are—not because their writers used exotic words—but rather because they used just the right words to describe the poignancy of their existences and the hope that Mrs. Roosevelt would help them.

In his "The History of the Profession" chapter in the *Handbook of Research on Teaching the English Language Arts* (1991, pp. 3–17), James Squire noted that textbooks dealing with writing instruction did not appear in American schools until the early nineteenth century. He observed, "As recently as 25 years ago, half of the Nation's high school teachers of English had not studied composition beyond freshman composition, and almost no elementary school teacher had formally studied language development or the teaching of writing" (p. 6). By 1992 all but 16 percent of eighth-grade teachers reported that they had received special training in teaching writing (Applebee, Langer, Mullis, Latham, & Gentile, 1994, p. 163). Proponents of the emphasis on total writing process have urged that spelling, grammar, usage, and other skill instruction be embedded in the process. What seemed to be missing in the earlier grammar/usage approaches to writing and in the more recent writing process methodologies is any serious attention to word selection within writing development. The *NAEP 1992 Writing Report Card* (Applebee et al., 1994) made no specific mention of the role of vocabulary or word selection anywhere within its 222 pages.

Flower and Hayes (1994) articulated a cognitive process theory of writing. In their model, they referred to three writing processes: planning, which includes goal setting and organizing; translating; and reviewing (p. 933).

Word selection comes into play during each of the three writing processes, and each word chosen is important. Flower and Hayes stated:

> As composing proceeds, a new element enters the task environment which places even more constraints upon what the writer can say. Just as a title constrains the content of a paper and a topic sentence shapes the options of a paragraph, each word in the growing text determines and limits the choices of what comes next. (p. 934)

The *New York Public Library Writer's Guide to Style and Usage* (1994) put it simply: "Good usage means using the right words at the right time for the right reasons" (p. 6).

Duin and Graves (1986, 1987, 1988) conducted a series of studies designed to investigate the effect of teaching vocabulary during prewriting on students' use of the words in their writing and on the quality of that writing. In a *Reading Research Quarterly* article (1987), they reported teaching 13 carefully selected words related to the theme "Space" to seventh graders. In Treatment 1, the 13 words were given varied and deep instruction that included questioning, discussing, recording, reading passages, using words in memos, noting words, and keeping log-books for six days. Activities included both vocabulary and writing tasks. Treatment 2 was identical to Treatment 1 but omitted writing activities. Treatment 3 incorporated vocabulary instruction using worksheets. Results showed that Treatment 1 subjects did best, followed by Treatment 2. Treatment 3 did least well on post-tests of vocabulary, judgments of writing quality, and measures of attitude toward the unit. The researchers concluded, "The central implication is that teaching a related set of words to students before they write an essay in which the words might be used can improve the quality of their essays" (p. 311).

Unless one is engaged in self-expressive writing, when one writes, one writes for a purpose and with a particular audience in mind. That audience and purpose shape the words selected. For example, scholarly writing involves appropriate technical jargon, fiction writers and song writers sometimes have an affinity for slang, and descriptive writing dictates the use of colorful words. Menu writers occasionally use overblown descriptions such as "Fresh fruit salad—transported in a pineapple boat for the highest vibration and your transmutation, with yogurt on the side for accent or dressing sprinkled with coconut . . . $6.35." This actual description was reported by Paul Dickson (1990, pp. 137–138). People who write for comedians have other challenges. Even an ordinary grocery list requires careful word selection if someone other than the writer or an immediate family member is to do the shopping.

## Choosing Words for Writing

*The difference between the right word and the almost right word is really a large matter. It's the difference between lightning and the lightning bug.*

—Mark Twain, 1888

Diction, that is, the writer's choice of words, is the heart of writing, having greater importance than even such other critical aspects of writing as sentence structure, paragraphing, and overall organization. Words are chosen because they serve a purpose. Words are chosen to signify objects, persons, ideas, feelings. They are chosen to influence the reader to do or believe something. They are chosen to establish the nature of the relationship between the writer and the reader that the writer desires. Kane (1988) referred to the different purposes words serve as "modes of meaning," and he has identified three such modes (p. 184).

The three modes of meaning are the referential, the interpersonal, and the directive.

**1.** Referential words connect the writer with the topic. Words are chosen for the precision with which they represent the meanings, thoughts, and feelings the writer wants to convey about the topic. Writers choose most words for their referential meanings—words that deal with the topic with exactness. For example, when writing about governments, words chosen to clarify an understanding of the executive, legislative, and judicial branches would be considered referential words by Kane.

**2.** Interpersonal words connect the writer with the reader, although even words chosen for their referential meanings serve to link the writer with the reader. Interpersonal words are selected based on what the writer assumes the readers do or do not know about the topic, the degree of formality the writer wants to establish, and the attitudes the writer wants the readers to have toward the writer. Words such as *I think* and *it seems to me* suggest modesty; words such as *we, our*, and *us* acknowledge the readers' presence. Words are in the interpersonal mode when they refer to the writer or the reader in those roles. Such words often are used when telling stories.

**3.** Directive words are chosen to help relate the readers to the topic. Words are selected that help readers understand or develop feelings about the topic. Words that facilitate understanding are called constructive diction, but words that evoke emotion are called emotive words. Words to facilitate understanding are chosen to help the reader follow the writer's logic, make connections, and clarify organization. Words such as *nonetheless, for example*, and *in the next section* are examples of constructive diction. Emotive diction aims at feelings, and such words especially are used in persuasive writing. Words that show bias, whether positive or negative, are examples (e.g., *reckless, overbearing, insightful, wise*).

A writer chooses some words needed to explain the topic (referential words); others are chosen to enhance the writer/reader relationship (interpersonal words), and still others to help the reader understand the topic or develop feelings about the topic (directive words). Kane (1988) concluded:

> You must, finally, realize that words inherently have meaning in some or in all of the modes we have enumerated. If you do not choose words wisely, words will, in effect, choose you, saying things about the topic you do not intend and affecting readers in ways you do not want. (p. 189)

How does a writer go about choosing "just the right word"? One tool that good writers make frequent use of is a thesaurus.

## The Thesaurus

People use a dictionary to check the meanings of words they do not know or are not sure about. They use a thesaurus, on the other hand, to select words that best express the meanings they have in mind. A thesaurus is primarily a book of synonyms. The entry words in a thesaurus, therefore, usually are more widely known than many dictionary entry words. In the foreword to *Webster's New World Thesaurus* (1985), Laird and Lutz state in their very first sentence, "This book is intended to help writers and speakers in search of a better way to say what they want to" (p. iii).

The first-known thesaurus was the *Erh Ya* compiled in China in about 800 B.C. Organized by topic headings, *Erh Ya* included correct usage of words as well as explanations of distinctions in their meanings. "It was compiled to help students of literature, and new editions were brought out until the 2nd century B.C." (Richardson, 1998, p. 16).

The name *Roget* has become synonymous with *thesaurus*. Roget originally did not set out to create a thesaurus of words and their synonyms to aid speakers and writers. He was a medical doctor who engaged in a lifetime hobby of trying to organize and classify all human knowledge. Roget developed six main categories of such knowledge: abstract relations, space, the material world, the intellect, volition, and sentient and moral powers. He subclassified these six into one thousand semantic subcategories, which became sections of Roget's well-known thesaurus (1852). The work was revised and the index greatly enlarged in 1854, and since then many revisions, new editions, and adaptations have been published. Although a brilliant accomplishment, Roget's thesaurus never was found to be the easiest reference to use. "Many a frustrated writer, seeking help in *Roget*, has found himself wandering in a maze where each turn of thought promises to produce the desired synonym, although none of them does" (Laird & Lutz, 1985, p. v). The major problem was one of access because Roget's thesaurus was organized by theme, not alphabetical order.

A second problem, and this might be true of all thesauri, has to do with the whole notion of synonymity. Strictly speaking, there are no words with identical meanings. Words may mean nearly the same thing, but may differ either in frequency (e.g., *tie, tether*), distribution (e.g., technical jargon such as *file* or *portfolio*), and connotation (e.g., *lectern, rostrum, pulpit*) (Rodale, Urdang, & LaRoche, 1986, introduction). Synonyms are words with similar but not the same meanings.

Most modern thesauri are alphabetically organized and for each entry word, the meanings, synonyms, related words, contrasting words, and antonyms often are included. Writers use thesauri to help them choose words of similar meaning, words stronger or weaker in force, words that are more formal or more folksy than the one in mind, idiomatic expressions that convey the same idea, or words that contrast or are opposite in meanings. Writers use a thesaurus to avoid using the same word repetitively, to try to find the exact word, or to try to jog loose a word stuck frustratingly on the tip of one's tongue. The thesaurus is an essential tool and constant companion of professional writers, and perhaps it ought to be for writers at all stages of development.

Thesauri are available for children and youth of all ages. *Words to Use* (Drysdale, 1974) was a children's thesaurus organized thematically in the same manner as Roget's original work. All of the included words were clustered within six broad, color-coded categories: The World We Live In, Living Things, Being Alive, How We View the World, Living Together, and Words for Sentence Building. The subcategories (e.g., The Senses) and subsubcategories (e.g., Hearing) were cleverly organized, illustrated, and displayed. The thesaurus included an index and instruction on its use. *Roget's Children's Thesaurus* (1994), intended for ages 8–12, and *Roget's Student Thesaurus* (1994), written for students ages 10–14, are representative of alphabetized thesauri for students. Included with entry words are the parts of speech, definitions, example sentences, synonyms, antonyms, and idioms. Some children's thesauri include other features such as word play, etymology, and writing tips.

## *Word Precision*

As the title of this chapter suggests, words must be precise if they are to be effective in serving the writer's purpose. Words must express exactly what the writer wants to convey to the reader. To choose words that express the writer's ideas or beliefs, words need to be used clearly and simply—not an easy task. There are several considerations that enter into a writer's word choice:

1. *Concrete-abstract.*    Concrete words usually signify unique, perceivable objects (e.g., *flagpole, hog, Louisiana Tech*), whereas abstract words signify concepts that cannot be directly perceived (e.g., *beauty, wealthy, unhealthy*). This is not to suggest that abstract words should be avoided by a writer; in certain kinds of writing and about particular topics, abstraction is desirable, even inevitable. The skillful writer helps readers who do not have topical expertise make sense of abstract words by using examples, analogies, similes, or metaphors to provide clarity. For example, understanding a writer's use of the concept *free and bound morphemes* can be simplified through the provision of examples (e.g., in *wanted* and *talking, want* and *talk* are *free* but *-ed* and *-ing* are without meaning unless they are *bound* to *want* and *talk*). Words are not either abstract or concrete; rather, they often exist on a continuum (e.g., *structure, building, residence, The White House*).

2. *Specific-general.*    A general word is a hypernym—it names a class (e.g., *seasoning*)—and specific words are hyponyms, or members of the class (e.g., *salt, pepper, chili powder, vinegar*). A specific word usually will give the reader a clearer understanding of what the writer intends than will a general word. For example, describing a salad as having arugula, endive, romaine, and vinaigrette gives a more descriptive picture than saying a salad has greens and seasonings.

3. *Ambiguous-explicit.*    Ambiguous words can be taken in more than one way in the context provided, but explicit words leave no doubt as to their meaning. Ambiguity often arises because so many words have more than one meaning as discussed in earlier chapters. In the sentence "The children were down in the dumps," is the intended meaning that the children were "feeling sad" or "in a landfill"? Anaphoric and cataphoric words may be ambiguous when it is not clear what words they are replacing or referring to. For example, in the sentences, "The Pelicans demolished the Cardinals. They couldn't get over it," we are left with ambiguity about who couldn't get over what. Careful writers try to create contexts that make explicit the intended meanings of potentially ambiguous words, for example, "The children were down in the dumps. They had never felt so brokenhearted." "The Pelicans demolished the Cardinals. This was the Cardinals' first loss and they couldn't get over it."

4. *Denotation-connotation.*    The denotation of a word shows the relationship between the word and its cognitive meaning. The connotation of a word includes the emotive associations suggested by the denotative meaning of the word. Connotations often imply approval or disapproval. For

example, *thrifty* and *frugal* connote someone who is sensible and watches pennies, but *cheap* and *tight* connote someone who is too miserly to part with any pennies. All four words denote someone who conserves money, but they connote very different feelings about such a person. Writers need to be aware of what the words they use connote as well as denote, or unintended messages may be sent.

**5.** *Informal-formal.* Colloquialisms and slang are two kinds of informal language. Pretentious English is the most extreme form of formal usage. The following short conversation (B. Johnson, 1995, p. 4) illustrates the difference.

Compare this:

> *Jan:* "Yo, Dean. Who's the bozo that just burned rubber outta here?"
>
> *Dean:* "The new neighbor. What a sponger! Came over to mooch more of my nails. They cost a pretty penny, too."

with this:

> *Jan:* "Hello, Dean. Who's the eccentric gentleman who left your driveway so rapidly?"
>
> *Dean:* "The new neighbor. He is taking advantage of my generosity. The fellow cajoled me out of more nails. They are quite expensive, too."

Which conversation is pretentious? In the second conversation, Jan and Dean sound like stuffed shirts. Generally speaking, colloquial and slang expressions are most appropriate to informal conversational occasions or when writing dialogue that captures such occasions. Writing usually requires use of more formal English. Shorter words typically lead to clearer understanding. Pretentiousness serves no purpose either in writing or speaking. Sometimes, though, unusual or uncommon words are necessary to the purpose of the writer.

**6.** *Clichés-jargon.* Clichés are overused expressions that have become dull and trite (e.g., *the bottom line, history tells us*); sometimes they are worn-out figures of speech (e.g., *happy as a lark, strong as an ox*). Jargon is technical language that is particular to a specialized trade, profession, or affinity group (e.g., some educators write about *constructivism, brain research, inclusion, induction*). Outside the specialized group that shares a common knowledge of the jargon, jargon becomes pretentious and even incomprehensible. The broad field of education is loaded with jargon unique to the profession (e.g., *whole language*) or with different meanings outside the profession (e.g., *scaffolding*). Good writers try to not use clichés and to use jargon only when writing technical information for appropriate readers.

7. *Barbarisms.*   Barbarisms are either words that do not exist or existing words that are used ungrammatically (e.g., "Marv said, 'I *suspicion* that most of our students have always wanted to be teachers.'" "I've never met such a self-assured, snobbish, *overborn* person."). Barbarisms should not be confused with neologisms, which are new words created for specific purposes. Barbarisms occur because writers are unclear about which suffix to use (e.g., *suspicion* for *suspect, overborn* for *overbearing*), or use improper or unnecessary prefixes (e.g., *irregardless* for *regardless*), or confuse the spellings of homophones (e.g., *great, grate; principle, principal*). Careful writers try to avoid barbarisms at all costs because readers take barbarisms as an indication of an unschooled or careless writer.

The challenge to writers, then, is to choose just the right words that will convey to readers the ideas the writer wants to convey—exactly, not vaguely. Often those "just right" words can be found within the writer's mental lexicon, but sometimes vocabulary resources such as a thesaurus are needed. When a writer is uncertain about whether a word will be understood by the likely reader, sufficiently rich context needs to be provided so that the word's meaning can be inferred.

## Revision

Most teachers give their students practice with some rendering of what is now called "the writing process." The steps in the process usually include prewriting (planning), drafting (writing), revising (reworking the piece), editing (fixing up spelling, punctuation, and usage), sharing (trying the piece out on others), and publishing (any formalized type of sharing). Tobin (1994) expressed concern that too great an emphasis on writing process has deemphasized the importance of the written product's form and correctness. Dahl and Farnan (1998) noted that many "real" writers do not follow the steps in the writing process because they follow their own individual procedures. Dahl and Farnan cited such writers as Flannery O'Connor, E. M. Forster, E. L. Doctorow, Beverly Cleary, Rosemary Sutcliff, and Jane Yolen as writers who engage in somewhat different processes as they write (pp. 15–17). It seems that process writing has become less popular with educators. Cassidy and Cassidy (December 1998–January 1999) conducted a survey of twenty-five "literacy leaders," asking their opinions about "what's hot and what's not" in the attention received by literacy educators. Seventy-five percent of those surveyed were of the opinion that process writing was "cold, not hot" at the end of the 1990s (p. 28).

What seems to be critical to writers—whether budding or accomplished—is the necessity for revision. Few writers are so gifted that they can write a piece that needs no revision. Just as there are relatively few gifted painters, musicians, and sculptors in this world, there are relatively small numbers of truly gifted writers. Even the very best writers need to revise and revise again to get a piece just right. Children who are learning to write also must learn to recognize the need for revision. The following conversation (Cheney, 1983, introduction) between George Plimpton of the *Paris Review* and Ernest Hemingway underscores this:

> **Paris Review:**   How much rewriting do you do?
>
> *Hemingway:*   It depends. I rewrote the ending to *A Farewell to Arms*, the last page of it, thirty-nine times before I was satisfied.
>
> **Paris Review:**   Was there some technical problem there? What was it that had stumped you?
>
> *Hemingway:*   GETTING THE WORDS RIGHT.

Marion Meade, in her biography *Dorothy Parker* (1987), reported that it was Parker's observation that Hemingway "was not the first novelist to rewrite a page sixty times" (p. 164). According to Cheney, "Seventy-five percent of all revision is eliminating words already written; the remaining twenty-five percent is improving the words that remain" (p. 1).

The purpose of writing is to communicate with a reader (unless expressing ourselves in a diary, personal journal, or note), so the writer must revise as much as necessary until confident that the intended meaning will be clear to the reader.

> It is this persistent search for the exact shade of meaning that makes the writer professional. If she feels that her vocabulary is not producing the just-right word, she doesn't hesitate to pore through the dictionary and the thesaurus until she finds it. (Cheney, p. 134)

In his biography of Truman Capote (1997), Plimpton related a conversation between Robert Ruark, the novelist who prided himself on writing several thousand words a day, and well-known writer Truman Capote.

> Ruark said, "I wrote five thousand words today, Truman, and I bet you sat there at that desk with your quill pen and wrote one word." Truman said, "Yes, Robert, but it was the *right* word," which was the best line I ever heard Truman get off. (p. 281)

Revision of a written piece is accomplished through three broad avenues: reduction, rearranging, and rewording. Reduction simply means getting rid of words, sentences, paragraphs, sections, or longer units that are superfluous, ineffective, or redundant. Rearranging is concerned with elements of unity (e.g., using consistent verb tenses), coherence (e.g., logical organization, parallel stucture), and emphasis (e.g., careful word choice). Rewording has to do with developing a personal style, paying attention to verbs (active rather than passive), using—not misusing—figurative language (e.g., metaphors, hyperbole), and correcting misspellings and incorrect uses.

Teachers develop their own approaches to teaching writing. Some follow traditional methods that stress elements of style and usage. Other teachers engage their students in writers' workshops (see Graves, 1983). Still others incorporate components of the writing process into their instruction. Whatever the approach to helping students become better writers, revision is an essential aspect. Revision need not be seen as drudgery or as simply giving the first draft "another quick glance." During revision, writers develop new insights into their work as well as feelings of pride from the awareness that they are polishing and improving their creation.

## Vocabulary and Writing Guidelines

The work of such researchers and theoreticians as Cheney (1983), Dahl and Farnan (1998), Fletcher (1993), and Kane (1988) allowed me to develop the following guidelines for vocabulary and writing.

**Guideline 1.** Numerous words are learned through rich oral language instruction and through wide reading. Learners continually expand their mental lexicons through oral language and reading as they mature, and these words all become available to them as they write.

**Guideline 2.** The prewriting stage of the writing process is critical. Using visual organizers such as the word webs described in the previous chapter can help young writers organize and outline their thoughts before they begin to write.

**Guideline 3.** When students engage in writing, encourage them to be active seekers of just the right words as they plan, compose, and especially as they revise.

### Teaching Suggestion

Choosing the right words through an activity called "fifty-five fiction." Read this little story:

*Wishful Thinking*

Bob had all he wanted. And he still had one wish left.

"I can't decide. Can I use it later?" he asked.

"You da boss. I'm just the genie."

"Cool."

As he walked down the streets, he searched for a tune to express his joyous feelings.

"Oh, I wish I were an Oscar Mayer wiener—" (Hanes, cited in Moss, 1995, 1998, p. 149)

Choosing "just the right words" is a task many writers find difficult; for most, it is easier to write a longer piece than a shorter one. Fifty-five fiction is the creation of Steve Moss who established a contest for writers. Their challenge was to write a short story using 55 words or fewer. Moss published the best of the submissions in a book titled *The World's Shortest Stories* (1995, 1998). Moss noted, "Fifty-five fiction is storytelling at its very leanest, where each word is chosen with utmost care on its way to achieving its fullest effect" (p. 7). Besides a "stingy word count," most writers plot their stories to involve a satisfying surprise ending such as what is about to happen to Bob in the story above.

Moss has developed a set of rules to guide writers of fifty-five fiction (pp. 219–222).

1. The pieces are to be fiction stories, not descriptions, opinions, poems, and so on.

2. The story, to be a story, must include four elements: setting, characters, conflict or problem, and a resolution or outcome. Some examples from "Wishful Thinking" are:

   *setting:* the time is the present, the place is the community

   *characters:* Bob and the genie

   *conflict or problem:* Bob has only one wish left

   *resolution or outcome:* The reader can infer what will happen to Bob as he sings the Oscar Mayer wiener song.

3. The writer can use fewer but not more than 55 words.

4. The title is not included in the 55 words.

5. Hyphenated words, acronyms, contractions, and numbers count as single words.

6. Punctuation marks do not count as words.

I have found that students in the upper elementary and middle grades are fascinated by the challenge of writing 55-word stories.

If any of your students write a "prize-winning" 55-word story, they may want to submit it for possible publication of the next "fifty-five fiction" book. Directions for submitting a story are included in Moss's book. Perhaps your class would like to publish its own little book of such stories written by creative class members. In addition to being both challenging and fun, creating a 55-word story makes clear to writers the importance of choosing just the right word.

**Guideline 4.** Students should be helped to understand that words serve purposes; among these purposes are referential words that connect the writer with the topic, interpersonal words that connect the writer with the reader, and directive words that connect the reader to the topic. When writing informational, descriptive, scholarly, or scientific papers, the writer-topic mode (referential) is most important, because the writer must carefully choose words that clearly explain the topic. Persuasive writing such as advertisements and political endorsements require added attention to the reader-topic mode (directive), because the writer must shape the opinions or actions of the reader toward the topic. Letter writing, storytelling, and personal experience accounts require writer-reader (interpersonal) connections through words that further the writer-reader bond. Many words, of course, will serve purposes in all three modes.

## Teaching Suggestion

Engage students in three types of writing to help them understand the different purposes words serve in writing. The 1998 National Assessment of Educational Progress test results showed that although only a small number of student responses were judged to be unsatisfactory, between one-fifth and one-half were judged below the sufficient level. The three types of writing assessed by NAEP are defined as follows:

> Informative writing focuses primarily on the subject matter element in communication and is used to share knowledge and to convey ideas. Narrative writing encourages students to incorporate their imagination and creativity into the production of stories or personal essays. Persuasive writing focuses on the reader, with the primary aim of influencing others to take some action or bring about change. (Greenwald et al., 1999, p. 4)

Providing your students with plenty of opportunities to write for the purposes of informing, narrating, and persuading will give them experience in selecting appropriate referential, interpersonal, and directive words. Such practice should stand them in good stead for the next NAEP assessment.

**Guideline 5.** Not every "just the right word" can be found in the writer's mental lexicon. A good thesaurus is often a writer's best friend, whether that writer is in elementary school or is an acclaimed novelist or Pulitzer prize winner. Students should be taught why, when, and how to use a thesaurus (explained in the front matter of most children or adult thesauri) and encouraged to develop the habit of having a thesaurus handy when writing. Ideally, each writer should have his or her own thesaurus and schools should provide classroom sets of a current and appropriate thesaurus. Familiarize students with larger thesauri and other word-finder books and resources available in the school media center, on CD-ROMs, and at pertinent Web sites.

## Teaching Suggestion

**Using a Thesaurus.**   Explain that a thesaurus is essentially a book of synonyms that presents other information as well. Using a thesaurus available in your school, teach your students how to understand a thesaurus entry. Figure 4.1 is a reprint of a sample entry used for instruction with *Roget's Student Thesaurus* (HarperCollins, 1994). Point out the entry word (e.g., *foolish*), definitions (e.g., *senseless, not wise*), example sentence (e.g., It was *foolish* of Gina to trust a stranger with her money), part of speech (adjective), synonyms (e.g., *silly, nonsensical, idiotic, absurd, preposterous, asinine*), cross-references (e.g., *crazy, stupid*), and antonyms (e.g., *sensible, wise*).

Demonstrate the other features of your thesaurus. They may include word stories, word play, word origins, tips for writers, quotations, idioms, figurative language, and vocabulary exercises. You may want to have your students revise one of their written works, using the thesaurus to help them achieve greater clarity, variety, and interest; more about revisions in Guideline 7. Encourage the regular use of a thesaurus when writing.

**Guideline 6.** When writing for an audience of readers, words should be precise if they are to be effective. Precision is facilitated when words are concrete, not abstract; specific, not general; explicit, not ambiguous; and when writers are aware of the connotations as well as the denotations of their words. Precision is facilitated when barbarisms, clichés, and inappropriate technical jargon are avoided. Writing is usually, but not always, more formal than speech. Students should be encouraged to use words in their written work that they wouldn't ordinarily use in their speech.

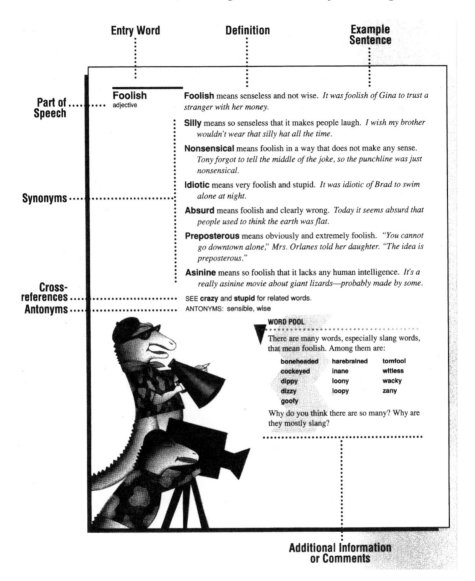

**Entry Word**

**Definition**

**Example Sentence**

**Part of Speech**

**Foolish**
adjective

**Foolish** means senseless and not wise. *It was foolish of Gina to trust a stranger with her money.*

**Silly** means so senseless that it makes people laugh. *I wish my brother wouldn't wear that silly hat all the time.*

**Nonsensical** means foolish in a way that does not make any sense. *Tony forgot to tell the middle of the joke, so the punchline was just nonsensical.*

**Synonyms**

**Idiotic** means very foolish and stupid. *It was idiotic of Brad to swim alone at night.*

**Absurd** means foolish and clearly wrong. *Today it seems absurd that people used to think the earth was flat.*

**Preposterous** means obviously and extremely foolish. *"You cannot go downtown alone," Mrs. Orlanes told her daughter. "The idea is preposterous."*

**Asinine** means so foolish that it lacks any human intelligence. *It's a really asinine movie about giant lizards—probably made by some.*

**Cross-references**
**Antonyms**

SEE **crazy** and **stupid** for related words.
ANTONYMS: sensible, wise

**WORD POOL**

There are many words, especially slang words, that mean foolish. Among them are:

| | | |
|---|---|---|
| boneheaded | harebrained | tomfool |
| cockeyed | inane | witless |
| dippy | loony | wacky |
| dizzy | loopy | zany |
| goofy | | |

Why do you think there are so many? Why are they mostly slang?

**Additional Information or Comments**

---

**FIGURE 4.1**   *How to Read a Thesaurus Entry*
*Roget's Student Thesaurus*, 1994, p. 9

## Teaching Suggestions

***1. Exemplify Abstract Concepts.***   One way to make abstract concepts become more concrete and easy to visualize is through the use of examples.

Have your students define an abstract concept such as *friendship* with an example or two similar to the following:

> "*Friendship* is saving a seat on the bus for my friend."
> "*Friendship* is being willing to listen."
> "*Friendship* is when you stand up for a person who is in trouble."

Here are some abstract concepts that you might want to use.

| | | |
|---|---|---|
| freedom | generosity | hope |
| hunger | evil | greed |
| understanding | helpful | justice |
| importance | success | prejudice |
| powerful | envy | criticism |
| honor | happiness | togetherness |

Students may pick a few of the abstract concepts that they understand and write definitions through exemplification. Then the class can share, compare, and discuss how the concrete examples brought the abstract concept to life.

***2. Bring Specificity to General Words and Ideas.***    General words are often class or category labels, and specific words provide detail about them. General words tend to be vaguer than specific words. Consider the word *soup*. It is a general class name. Next, consider *homemade soup*. *Homemade* adds some specificity because we have learned the soup probably did not come out of a can. Still greater specificity is added in the following example: "Thick, rich, homemade chicken noodle soup seasoned with just a hint of rosemary." The chicken noodle soup has become so visible that the reader can almost smell and taste it. Ask your students to provide specificity by writing descriptive sentences or paragraphs related to the following general statements.

    **a.** There was a traffic jam on Friday.
    **b.** California has a more diverse population than some other states.
    **c.** The breakfast cereal is interesting.
    **d.** Shaundra has great qualities.
    **e.** The landscape in Maine is quite varied.
    **f.** The spring rolls were tasty.
    **g.** Jackson has different types of housing.
    **h.** The bad disease spread rapidly.

 i. We watched the holiday parade.
 j. In middle school there are a lot of extracurricular activities.

Writers who want to help their readers clearly understand their message will be sure to deal in specificities, not generalities. Your students may enjoy comparing the descriptions they have written.

*3. Clarifying Ambiguities Through Explicit Writing.* The English lexicon contains thousands of multiple-meaning words. Each word that has more than one meaning is potentially ambiguous to the reader, unless the writer is careful to provide sufficiently rich context to eliminate the ambiguity. The following list of ambiguous "newspaper headlines" exemplifies this. Have your students discuss the possible alternative meanings of the headlines. Then have them rewrite the headlines or add additional words or sentences to do away with the ambiguity.

 a. Community Acts on Town Dump
 b. Store Loses Inventory of Speakers
 c. Fish Biting off Gulf Coast
 d. Governor Puts Blame on Dense Population
 e. Rash Decisions Annoy Hospital Personnel
 f. Boat Drawing Today
 g. Rose to Speak at Garden Club
 h. Monarchs Appear in Local Gardens
 i. Restaurant Famous for Its Cobbler
 j. Jury Hears Testimony in Tuba Case
 k. Local Man Cited in Author's Appendix
 l. Attorney Presents Argument in Circus Suit

Students can scour local newspapers and news magazines for more ambiguous headlines. Sports pages are particularly fertile. Discussion and writing to clarify ambiguity will help your students be alert to possible ambiguity in their own writing.

**Guideline 7.**  Help your students develop the habit of revision. Most revision results in the elimination of words already written. In addition to such reduction, revision comes through rearranging and rewording what has been written for purposes of style, clarity, and accuracy. The best advice to beginning writers is to write a first draft as quickly as it will flow, then to revise at leisure. Revision takes time but it can be rewarding as the writer strives to help the reader understand, feel, and act as she wants.

*Teaching Suggestion*

*Eliminate Words.*    Most revision of what has been written is accomplished by eliminating words. Novice writers sometimes make the mistake of redundancy, that is, saying the same thing more than once when repetition has not been deliberately included for effect. Often the reduction can be accomplished by omitting just a word or two. Have your students work in pairs examining sentences such as the following. Their task is to agree on the words that can be eliminated without changing the intent of the sentence. Possible words for deletion are found in parentheses.

1. At 3:00 P.M. in the afternoon it began to snow. *(in the afternoon)*
2. The detective said he was only interested in true facts, not opinions. *(only, true)*
3. They expected a sellout but just a few in number showed up. *(in number)*
4. Those two paragraphs have the same identical meaning. *(identical)*
5. Twenty dollars a week was the maximum possible amount she could save. *(possible)*
6. The swimming class was made up of fifteen new beginners. *(new)*
7. Test scores showed a range all the way from zero to one hundred. *(all the way)*
8. I was elated when the puzzle was entirely completed. *(entirely)*
9. She enjoys the opera every now and then. *(every)*
10. The sky was a beautiful blue in color. *(in color)*

Now see if your students can spot redundancies in paragraphs such as the one that opened this Teaching Suggestion (of what has been written, for effect). Next, classmates can examine works they have written to find redundancies that could be eliminated. *Deep Revision: A Guide for Teachers, Students, and Other Writers* (Willis, 1993) contains numerous revision exercises, and many ideas for making writing fresher and richer through revision.

**Guideline 8.**   Help your budding writers develop a love of words. Unless they can become "word freaks," they will not be capable of their best writing. The final chapter is filled with ways to get young learners interested in words.

With an ever-expanding English lexicon of more than two million words, learning to locate words and meanings has become more vital than ever, and that is the focus of the next chapter.

*References* _____

Applebee, A. N., Langer, J. A., Mullis, I. V. S., Latham, A. S., & Gentile, C. A. (1994). *NAEP 1992 writing report card*. Washington, D.C.: U.S. Department of Education.

Carroll, J. B., Davies, P., & Richman, B. (1971). *The American Heritage word frequency book*. Boston: Houghton Mifflin.

Cassidy, J., & Cassidy, D. (1998/1999, December/January). What's hot, what's not for 1999. *Reading Today*, pp. 1, 28.

Cheney, T. A. R. (1983). *Getting the words right: How to rewrite, edit & revise*. Cincinnati, OH: Writer's Digest Books.

Cohen, R. (1996). Dear Mrs. Roosevelt: Cries for help from Depression youth. *Social Education, 60* (5), 271–276.

Dahl, K. L., & Farnan, N. (1998). *Children's writing: Perspectives from research*. Newark, DE: International Reading Association.

Dickson, P. (1990). *Slang! Topic-by-topic dictionary of American lingoes*. New York: Pocket Books.

Drysdale, P. (1974). *Words to use: A junior thesaurus*. New York: William H. Sadlier.

Duin, A. H., & Graves, M. F. (1986). Effects of vocabulary instruction used as prewriting technique. *Journal of Research and Development in Education, 20* (Fall), 7–13.

Duin, A. H., & Graves, M. F. (1987). Intensive vocabulary instruction as a prewriting technique. *Reading Research Quarterly, 22* (3), 311–330.

Duin, A. H., & Graves, M. F. (1988). Teaching vocabulary as a writing prompt. *Journal of Reading, 32*, 204–212.

Fletcher, R. (1993). *What a writer needs*. Portsmouth, NH: Heinemann.

Flower, L., & Hayes, J. R. (1994). A cognitive process theory of writing. In R. B. Ruddell, M. R. Ruddell, & H. Singer (Eds.), *Theoretical models and processes of reading* (4th ed., pp. 928–950). Newark, DE: International Reading Association.

Graves, D. H. (1983). *Writing: Teachers and children at work*. Portsmouth, NH: Heinemann.

Hillerich, R. L. (1978). *A writing vocabulary of elementary children*. Springfield, IL: Charles C. Thomas.

Horn, E. (1926). A basic writing vocabulary: 10,000 words most commonly used in writing. *University of Iowa Monographs in Education* (First Series, No. 4).

Indrisano, R., & Squire, J. R. (Eds.). (2000). *Perspectives on writing: Research, theory, and practice*. Newark, DE: International Reading Association.

Johnson, B. v. H. (1995). Figurative language: Nothing to sneeze at. *The Reading Professor, 17* (2), 4–12.

Johnson, D. D. (Ed.). (1986). Vocabulary [Special issue]. *Journal of Reading, 29* (7).

Kane, T. S. (1988). *The new Oxford guide to writing*. Oxford, UK: Oxford University Press.

Kucera, H., & Francis, W. N. (1967). *Computational analysis of present-day American English*. Providence, RI: Brown University Press.

Laird, C., & Lutz, W. D. (1985). *Webster's new world thesaurus*. New York: Simon & Schuster.

Meade, M. (1987). *Dorothy Parker*. New York: Penguin Books.

Moe, A. J., Hopkins, C. J., & Rush, R. T. (1982). *The vocabulary of first-grade children*. Springfield, IL: Charles C. Thomas.

Moss, S. (1995, 1998). *The world's shortest stories*. Philadelphia, PA: Running Press.

Murphy, H. A. (1957). Spontaneous speaking vocabulary of children in primary grades. *Journal of Education, 140*, 1–104.

*New York Public Library writer's guide to style and usage*. (1994). New York: HarperCollins.

Plimpton. G. (1997). *Truman Capote*. New York: Nan A. Talese.

Richardson, M. (1998). *Whose bright idea was that?* New York: Kodansha International.

Rinsland, H. D. (1945). *A basic vocabulary of elementary school children*. New York: The Macmillan Company.

Rodale, J. I., Urdang, L., & LaRoche, N. (1986). *The synonym finder*. New York: Warner Books.

Roget, P. M. (1852). *Thesaurus of English words and phrases classified and arranged so as to facilitate the expression of ideas and assist in literary composition*. New York: Thomas Y. Crowell.

*Roget's children's thesaurus*. (Rev. ed.). (1994). New York: HarperCollins.

*Roget's student thesaurus*. (Rev. ed.). (1994). New York: HarperCollins.

Squire, J. R. (1991). The history of the profession. In J. Flood, J. M. Jensen, D. Lapp, & J. R. Squire (Eds.), *Handbook of research on teaching the English language arts* (pp. 3–17). New York: Macmillan.

Thorndike, E. L. (1931). *The teacher's word book of 20,000 words*. New York: Teachers College, Columbia University.

Thorndike, E. L., & Lorge, I. (1944). *The teacher's word book of 30,000 words*. New York: Teachers College, Columbia University.

Tobin, L. (1994). Introduction: How the writing process was born—and other conversion narratives. In L. Tobin & T. Newkirk (Eds.), *Taking stock: The writing process movement in the '90s*. Portsmouth, NH: Boynton/Cook.

U.S. Department of Education. Office of Educational Research and Improvement. National Center for Education Statistics. The NAEP 1998 Writing Report Card for the Nation and the States, NCES 1999-462, by E. A. Greenwald, H. R. Persky, J. R. Campbell, and J. Mazzeo. Washington, D.C.: 1999.

Willis, M. S. (1993). *Deep revision: A guide for teachers, students, and other writers*. New York: Teachers and Writers Collaboration.

# 5

## *Where Words Are Stored*

### *The Dictionary and Other References*

*No dictionary of a living tongue ever can be perfect, since while it is hastening to publication, some words are budding and some falling away.*

—Samuel Johnson, 1755

Dictionaries and thesauri have different purposes, provide somewhat different information, and often are organized differently. A dictionary is used by someone, usually a reader or listener, who wants to look up a word to find out its meaning, spelling, or pronunciation. A thesaurus more frequently is used by a writer or speaker who is looking for a better way to express an idea. A dictionary is a book of word meanings (and multiple meanings called "senses" by lexicographers), spellings, pronunciations, grammatical information, and sometimes etymologies and illustrative usages. A thesaurus primarily is a book of synonyms that, for some words, presents antonyms, related words, and even definitions and grammatical information. A dictionary is organized alphabetically; a thesaurus may be organized either by topics (see Dutch, 1965) or alphabetically (see Webster, 1976). The thesaurus was described and exemplified in the preceding chapter on vocabulary and writing. The dictionary will be the primary focus of the present chapter.

In the Fall of 1998, a book documenting a story of murder and insanity began to appear in independent bookstores in North America. Before long, the volume had begun to show up on the best-seller lists of the *New York*

*Times* and *Publishers Weekly*. It climbed to near the top of the nonfiction lists where it remained for months in late 1998 and 1999. That a murder story became a best seller was nothing new, but the topic of this book indicates why it became a surprise best seller. *The Professor and the Madman: A Tale of Murder, Insanity, and the Making of the Oxford English Dictionary* (Winchester, 1998) tells the tale of Dr. James Murray, the first editor of the *Oxford English Dictionary* (1928) and Dr. William Chester Minor, an American surgeon who had served as a Union officer in the Civil War. Minor had been convicted of murdering an Englishman in 1875 and was confined in Broadmoor, England's most feared asylum for "criminal lunatics" (p. xi).

The book also is the story of the creation of the *Oxford English Dictionary*, a seventy-year undertaking from conceptualization to final publication. The *Dictionary* "is recognized throughout the world as the most complete historical record of the English language ever assembled" (Berg, 1993, p. vii). Dr. Murray was a noted lexicographer who was invited by the Delegates of the Oxford University Press to lead the development of a new, comprehensive dictionary. Murray and his team of compilers recruited thousands of "readers" whose job it was to read the entirety of English literature and select sentence-length illustrations of every sense of every word in the English language. This was an astonishing task in those days long before computers when everything had to be recorded by hand on small slips of paper and mailed to Dr. Murray. Dr. William Minor, the "criminal lunatic," became one of the readers and eventually was the most prolific, contributing more than 10,000 neat, handwritten quotations he had located from his "home" in Broadmoor asylum.

This remarkable, best-selling, nonfiction account of a distinguished lexicographer, a brilliant but incarcerated literary researcher, and the development of the world's greatest dictionary, stimulated a revived interest in words, the *OED (Oxford English Dictionary)*, and other dictionaries at the end of the twentieth century.

## Historical Background

Dictionaries have been in existence since about 2,000 B.C., but as we now know them, they are relatively recent reference compilations. There were no English language dictionaries, for example, when the most famous poet and playwright of the English language, William Shakespeare, was writing his 150 sonnets and more than 35 plays, including *The Taming of the Shrew* (1592), *As You Like It* (1599), and *Hamlet* (1601). Shakespeare could not do what writers today can do when they have a question about a word's meaning, spelling, or pronunciation. Shakespeare could not look it up in the dictionary.

The very earliest dictionaries were bilingual or "polyglot" dictionaries whose purpose was to help travelers translate one language into another.

> The earliest bilingual dictionary was a Sumerian-Akkadian dictionary produced in Mesopotamia on clay tablets in about 2,000 B.C. About 500 years later a Sumerian-Babylonian-Hittite dictionary was probably the world's first trilingual dictionary. (Richardson, 1998, p. 15)

The first dictionary to become a precursor to modern English dictionaries was a dictionary of Chinese characters compiled in about 100 A.D. by Hsew Shen and titled *Explaining Words, Analyzing Characters*. It analyzed 9,353 different characters in terms of the meanings and pronunciations of their constituent parts. This dictionary has been in constant use for 1,900 years (Richardson, p. 15).

Credit for the first monolingual English language dictionary is given to Robert Cawdrey for his *A Table Alphabeticall . . . of Hard Unusual English Words* (1604). Its 2,500 word entries were defined in a slim 120-page volume. Cawdrey did not attempt to be comprehensive and included only words he thought to be difficult or rarely used. Two other English language dictionaries became famous before the publication of the *OED*. Dr. Samuel Johnson, the famous English lexicographer, compiled the *Dictionary of the English Language* (1755). It took nine years of work by Johnson and his team to complete the two-volume dictionary. Information for each entry word included meanings, spellings, pronunciations, morphology, idiomatic expressions, and illustrative quotations from the literature for every sense of every word. The word *take*, for example, contained supportive quotations for 134 different senses (e.g., *grasp, capture, win, indulge in, select, accept*). Johnson's dictionary provided comprehensive treatment of 43,500 entry words and used 118,000 illustrative quotations. The *American Dictionary of the English Language* by Noah Webster (1824) was compiled as an American "replacement" for Samuel Johnson's work. Webster was intensely nationalistic—the United States was a very young nation—and he was critical of Johnson's word choices and spellings. Webster wrote his own illustrative sentences for the words rather than using literary quotations from English authors. He wanted American English to have its own dictionary. Miller (1996), however, observed, "Historians have judged it a minor contribution to lexicography that would have disappeared had it not been actively promoted and heavily revised by its publishers" (p. 139).

The most acclaimed English dictionary is the *Oxford English Dictionary* (1928). Work on the *Dictionary* began in 1857, and the first edition was published in 128 "fascicles" (installments, e.g., *a* to *ant, anta* to *battening*) between 1884 and 1928. It was published in its entirety in 10 volumes in 1928 and reissued in 12 volumes in 1933. The *OED* defined 414,800 word forms and used 1,861,200 quotations to illustrate word senses. Of the 2,700 authors represented in the quotations, Shakespeare was cited most (33,500 citations). Four supplements were issued between 1972 and 1986, and they added 69,300 more entries and 527,000 additional quotations. A 20-volume second edition of *OED* was published in 1989. Within its 21,730 pages, it defined 615,100 word forms and used 2,436,600 quotations (Berg, 1993, pp. 194–195). The *OED* is a diachronic dictionary that defines words not only in terms of present-day usage but also documents historical changes in their uses through cited illustrative quotations. In contrast, synchronic dictionaries present only information and examples from present-day use. The Webster dictionary and its offshoots were synchronic dictionaries. The second edition of *OED* became available on CD-ROMs in 1992 and 1993. A third edition of the *Oxford English Dicitonary* is scheduled for completion in 2010, but most of it will be available through the Internet before then.

The most recent development in dictionary publication is the *Encarta World English Dictionary* (1999). It was the first entirely new dictionary to be compiled from all the main national varieties of English. Composed of more than 3,000,000 words derived from a single 50,000,000-word database of world English, its publication in both American and British editions as well as on CD-ROM and the Internet make it a unique lexicographical contribution. Its goal is to define English as the world's first global language; it includes words from the Internet, international business, and worldwide science and technology. Spin-offs planned include both student and single-topic dictionaries.

## *Kinds of Dictionaries*

Dictionaries broadly can be categorized into four types: monolingual general dictionaries of a language, bilingual or multilingual dictionaries used for translation, single-function dictionaries such as pronouncing, rhyming, reverse, visual, or spelling dictionaries, and single-topic dictionaries such as dictionaries of proverbs or medical terms, and many more. See Figure 5.1.

Dictionaries may also be categorized according to their intended audiences, for example, the general public, college, high school, middle school, elementary school, or preschool students, members of professions, subject specialists, browsers, and so on. Some dictionaries primarily use pictures to portray meanings, some use schematic drawings, but most use words, abbreviations, diacritical marks, and illustrations. The two factors that determine whether or not someone might find a dictionary interesting and helpful are coverage and treatment. Coverage refers to the number and types of entry words included in the dictionary. Treatment means the kind of information provided for each entry word. Differences in coverage and treatment can be seen within the four types of dictionaries described next.

FIGURE 5.1 *Four Kinds of Dictionaries*

| Kind | Purpose | Example |
|---|---|---|
| General Dictionaries | Present an alphabetized list of words, together with pronunciations, function, meaning, and more | *Encarte World Dictionary* |
| Bilingual or Multilingual Dictionaries | Present a list of words and meanings in two or more languages used by translators and tourists | *Langenscheidts Taschenwoerterbuch* |
| Single-function Dictionaries | Present only one type of information about a list of words, such as their pronunciations, spellings, or illustrations | *Bernstein's Reverse Dictionary* |
| Single-topic Dictionaries | Presents words and their meanings that fall in one category such as proverbs, idioms, or medicine | *Oxford Dictionary of English Grammar* |

The monolingual general dictionaries are the most commonly used dictionaries, and they come in all sizes from small paperbacks to twenty-volume sets. A monolingual general dictionary is a reference book that contains an alphabetized list of entry words and for each entry presents the spelling, pronunciation, grammatical status, meanings of the different senses of the word, history, illustrative sentences, and inflected forms. A good dictionary should give the meanings of any word that needs to be understood, the spelling of any word that needs to be written, and the pronunciation of any word that needs to be spoken. Examples of such dictionaries are those described earlier that were compiled by Samuel Johnson, Noah Webster, and James Murray. All of these dictionaries have gone through a number of revisions.

Bilingual and multilingual dictionaries are used by persons learning a foreign language, by translators, and sometimes by tourists. An example of a bilingual dictionary is *Langenscheidts Taschenwoerterbuch: English* (Klatt, Roy, Klatt, & Messinger, 1983). It presents an alphabetized list of English words with their pronunciations, along with their synonyms and definitions in German. This English-German reference comprises the first 600 pages. The remaining 700 pages present an alphabetized list of German words and their pronunciations, and then synonyms and definitions in English—a German-English reference. The work can be used profitably by native speakers of either English or German.

There are several kinds of single-function dictionaries. Pronouncing dictionaries give, for each entry word, only pronunciations using a phonetic alphabet and diacritical marks. When words have variant pronunciations (e.g., *apricot, greasy, suite*), the most common pronunciation precedes the less common. Such a dictionary is of interest to linguists, people who care about correct speech, and anyone wanting to settle an argument about how a word is pronounced. An example is *A Pronouncing Dictionary of American English* (Kenyon & Knott, 1953), a favorite reference book of linguists for 50 years. Rhyming dictionaries are especially useful to poets, songwriters, and teachers preparing rhyming activities for their students. Such dictionaries are organized through alphabetization of the final rhyming sounds of words—not by the spellings. After each final sound is a list of words containing that sound (e.g., /arm/: *arm, charm, farm, harm, alarm*; /ooth/: *Ruth, booth, couth, sleuth, tooth, Duluth*). (Please see the following Teaching Suggestion for a recommended rhyming dictionary.)

Reverse dictionaries (e.g., *Bernstein's Reverse Dictionary*, 1975), another type of single-function dictionary, are organized by alphabetized word meanings, and for each meaning, words and synonyms that represent that meaning are given. Such dictionaries are of some use when the word is on the tip of the tongue, when we know what we want to say but can't come up with the right word. A good thesaurus or book of synonyms will serve the same purpose. Visual dictionaries use illustrations and detailed drawings to indicate a word's meaning or how a device or gadget functions. Their focus is usually on technical words. Computer spell-check programs have largely replaced spelling dictionaries, which are organized by plausible erroneous spellings and were once popular with typists and stenographers.

## Teaching Suggestion

There is a good chance that your school library will have at least one rhyming dictionary on its shelves. One that I have found to be helpful is *The New Comprehensive American Rhyming Dictionary* (1991) compiled by Sue Young. Rhyming is fun, and it can be easy if the student has access to resources. To get your students interested in rhyming, share with them some hink pink and hinky pinky riddles such as the following:

> What do you call a warm kettle? (a hot pot)
> What is a quick explosion? (a fast blast)
> How would you describe a tiny shopping center? (a small mall)
> Which is the aging rock? (the older boulder)
> What do you call a skinny horse? (a bony pony)
> Who gives support to a chicken? (a rooster booster)

The challenge for your class is to create some hink pink or hinky pinky riddles (see Chapter 9 for descriptions and examples) by using a rhyming dictionary as a reference. A rhyming dictionary will reveal that under the /eye/ sound, for example, many words are available, including *buy, cry, eye, high, tie,* and so on. A student might create, "What do you call a thirsty insect?" (a dry fly). After students have had a chance to think of a hink pink or two, alone or in groups, they can try to stump their classmates. In the process, they will discover the fun of rhyming and the value of a rhyming dictionary.

The fourth major category of dictionaries includes the thousands of single-topic dictionaries in existence. Works abound in every field from accounting to ceramics, dentistry, geology, psychology, photography, and even the ships of the world. Within most academic fields, a number of highly specialized dictionaries have been compiled. In doing my research for the book you are now reading, for example, I consulted nearly one hundred different specialized, single-topic dictionaries on more than two dozen topics related to the general category "vocabulary." The topics were:

### Twenty-Five Single-Topic Dictionaries Related to "Vocabulary"

**1.** *Acronyms and abbreviations.* These are words formed from the initial letter or letters of a group of words, or they are shortened forms of words. Examples: *e-mail, phys ed, NATO, MADD, r.s.v.p., Mr.*

**2.** *Aphorisms.* Aphorisms are maxims or adages, tersely worded truths or opinions such as *A stumble may prevent a fall.*

**3.** *Catchphrases.* A catchphrase is a phrase that appeals to the public and is in frequent use for a period of time. Examples: *Have a nice day; been there, done that; Go for it.*

**4.** *Changes in meaning.* Some dictionaries contain only words that have rather significantly changed in meaning over time. For example, the word *shroud,* now associated with death, formerly meant simply *a garment.*

**5.** *Clichés.* Clichés are trite expressions (e.g., similes or idioms) that have been overused and are found to be tiresome. Examples: *as smooth as glass, as green as grass, costs a pretty penny, water under the bridge.*

**6.** *Confusibles.* Dictionaries of confusables present pairs of words that often are interchanged and thus misused by speakers and writers. Examples: *affect-effect, infer-imply, two-to-too.*

**7.** *Cultural literacy.* Words, phrases, famous individuals, slogans, and song titles all comprise cultural literacy, what someone thinks an educated person ought to know. For example, knowledge of *Picasso, Mother Goose rhymes, poetry genres, Appomattox,* and *note bene* are thought to be part of our cultural literacy according to one such dictionary (Hirsch, 1988).

**8.** *Doublespeak.* Doublespeak is language that is used for purposes of evasion or ambiguity (e.g., *conflict* for *war, emerging nation* for *an underdeveloped country, cash flow problem* for *no money*).

**9.** *English language.* A dictionary of the English language details words that explain the structure, phonology, lexicon, and literature of the language. Sample entries might include *Leonard Bloomfield, mixed metaphor, spelling reform.*

**10.** *Eponyms and toponyms.* Eponyms are words derived from the names of real persons, and toponyms are words derived from the names of places. Examples include *martinet, Ferris wheel, watt, Brussels sprouts, plaid.*

**11.** *Etymology.* Etymology is the history and development of word structures and meanings. For example, *malapropism* is a word derived from a character in a play (Mrs. Malaprop in *The Rivals*) that came into use in about 1849.

**12.** *Euphemisms.* A euphemism is a socially acceptable word used in place of a word that makes some people uncomfortable in some way (e.g., *passed away* for *died, expecting* for *pregnant, creative* for *false*).

**13.** *First names.* A first name is the name given to a child at birth, usually by the parents. First names are selected from every imaginable source including ancestors, the Bible, famous people, flowers, months, and so on. Examples: *Aaron, Aisha, April, Luke, Maria, Rose, Ryan.*

**14.** *Foreign words.* Foreign words are those words that have been adopted into English use from another language. They include such words as *coma, filet, lager, kindergarten, shish-kabob, trio.*

**15.** *Grammar.* A dictionary of grammar defines all the words used to explain any aspect of the grammar of a language. Examples: *clause, gerund, dialect, genitive, zeugma.*

**16.** *Idioms.* There are numerous dictionaries of idioms: general, American, African, German, and so on. An idiom is an expression whose meaning is not the same as the meanings of the individual words within the expression. Examples: *to be in hot water, to come down to earth,* and *to wear more than one hat.*

**17.** *Linguistics.* A dictionary of linguistics defines all the words and jargon used in any of the subspecialties of linguistics. Included are such words as *allophone, glottal, sociolinguistics, morphophonemic, diachronic, lexeme.*

**18.** *Literacy.* Words related to any aspect of literacy development are likely to be found in such a dictionary. Words included in a literacy dictionary are *phonics, critical literacy, vocabulary, cursive, expository, metacognition.*

**19.** *Place names.* These are the names of specific locations such as *Ruston, De Pere, Dublin, Louisiana, Wisconsin, Ireland.*

**20.** *Proverbs.* A proverb is a wise saying expressing a truth or a viewpoint. Examples: *Too many cooks spoil the broth; Eat to live, don't live to eat.* The seeker of proverbs will find a large number of dictionaries from which to choose.

**21.** *Quotations.* A quotation is the citation of a statement spoken or written by another person. For example, this quotation from Samuel Johnson in 1755 is frequently cited: *"Lexicographer: a writer of dictionaries, a harmless drudge."*

**22.** *Slang.* Slang is informal speech in the form of words or phrases best known to members of common-interest groups or professions. Numerous dictionaries of slang are available. Slang examples include *to make a bundle, geek, duck squeezer.*

**23.** *Surnames.* A surname is a person's family name as distinguished from the given or first name. Surnames may indicate ethnic background, ancestral employment, place of origin, or others. Some surnames are *Weinberg, Garnet, Cai, Nurmi, Baker.*

**24.** *Word games.* Several dictionaries present alphabetized and categorized lists of word- and language-play games together with their descriptions and rules of play. Example games include *acrostics, Brain Train, twenty questions, anagrams.*

**25.** *Word origins.* Word origins are word histories that are not as technical as etymologies. Dictionaries of origins typically tell the interesting stories behind such words as *grandfather's clock, tin ear, windfall.*

More than two dozen different subcategories of single-topic dictionaries about the general topic "vocabulary" exist. Some categories such as idioms, proverbs, and slang offer a rather large variety of high quality, scholarly dictionaries compiled by specialized researchers and lexicographers. Vocabulary is just one of the many topics pertinent to the broader category of "language." No wonder that thousands of dictionaries of these four types—general, bilingual, single-function, and single-topic—have been published. There is no shortage of dictionaries in the land. Crystal (1997) stated, "Since the 1970s, the flow of dictionaries has been unabated, as publishers try to meet the needs of an increasingly language-conscious age" (p. 111).

## Teaching Suggestions

**1.** Arrange for a class visit to the school library or media center for the purpose of introducing your students to available vocabulary references. The librarian or specialist could be asked to give a "book talk" demonstrating and explaining the various dictionaries and thesauri that are there. The library probably will have a good variety of general, bilingual, single-function, and single-topic dictionaries of high quality. The tour and demonstration should include CD-ROM dictionaries and reference suites as well as printed dictionaries. Most librarians are happy to give such demonstrations, because the knowledge enables students to make use of these valuable reference works.

2. Comparing dictionaries can be an informative activity for young learners. Select one or two large dictionaries from the school library, perhaps a smaller pocket dictionary, and the dictionary set available in your classroom. Have your students decide which word to compare in the dictionaries. First the students can locate the word in their classroom dictionary and read the entry information. Next, volunteers can look up the same word in the pocket dictionary and in the larger general dictionaries. Your class probably will find it notable that even the large dictionaries vary somewhat in their coverage of a word. The differences may be in total coverage, specific definitions, illustrations, slang, variant spellings, or other elements. Repeat the exercise with more words. The purpose of the activity is to help your students realize that some dictionaries are just more useful than others, so it may be necessary, at times, for them to consult more than one dictionary.

## School Dictionaries

School dictionaries are in no short supply for those teachers, parents, or school-purchasing agents in the market for them. Picture dictionaries compiled for preschoolers are available from nearly every publisher of children's books and school textbooks. The same is true for students in the primary grades, middle school, and high school. Numerous dictionaries for children and youth ages 3–18 are available, and dozens more exist for college students. Perhaps the best way to survey the children and adolescent's dictionaries currently available in print is to check an on-line bookstore. Web-based bookstores, such as Amazon (www.Amazon.com), stock and maintain a vast list of books for youth including dictionaries and other reference works. In 1999, Amazon listed 483 titles under the search "children's dictionaries."

The newest dictionaries have inviting formats and captivating visuals to make their use pleasing to the eye and enjoyable to use. They have become increasingly multicultural in recognition of the growing diversity in American schools. There now are more children with non-European backgrounds in classrooms. The new dictionaries' bibliographical entries include more Native Americans, Latinos, African Americans, and women. In recognition of the larger number of non-native English speakers, lexicographers recently have written more helpful definitions for idioms because of major problems idioms can present for such learners.

Some new dictionaries provide brief descriptions of the origins of some words. The explanations show that although most English words have Latin and Greek roots, an expanding number of words spring from African, Asian, Caribbean, and Native American roots as well as from the Indian subcontinent, Australia, and New Zealand. The dictionaries give comprehensive treatment to inoffensive, established slang words, because they are an important part of the language. Slang selection is not an easy task for a lexicographer, because slang is ever-evolving, and some slang words exist only briefly or just in certain locales (e.g., Valley girls' slang from the San Fernando Valley of California in the 1980s: *gnarly, raspy, cril, grody*).

The best student dictionaries contain easy-to-use pronunciation guides, easy-to-understand definitions, precise explanations of grammar and usage, engrossing origins of words, and much more. The front matter of the dictionary exists to give students and teachers information about how to use the dictionary. Included there are examples and sometimes instructional and practice activities that help users become familiar with the dictionary. The following is a list of the sections typically provided in the front matter of a dictionary to give students a complete and helpful picture of the work.

### Sections Found in School Dictionary Front Matter

**1.** *Organization of the dictionary.* This component describes the kinds of information that can be found in the dictionary, where information is located, the use of color coding or boldface type, the functions of illustrations and maps, and descriptions of the special sections of the dictionary.

**2.** *Alphabetical order.* This section discusses the way words can be accessed in the dictionary, first by initial letter (e.g., *apple, banana*), then by second letter (e.g., *goat, guppy*), third (e.g., *dense, dentist*), fourth (e.g., *snap, snare*), and so on.

**3.** *Guide words.* This part explains that there are two words at the top of each page, usually highlighted in some way. The word on the left is the first entry word on that page and the word on the right is the last entry word on the page. By using alphabetical order, and the guide words, students can tell at a glance if the word they are looking for is on that page.

**4.** *Entry words.* This segment tells what information the student can expect to find for each entry word in the dictionary. The usual parts of an entry, besides the obvious spelling of the word, include the definition, meanings of the different senses of the word (e.g., to feel *faint*, to hear a *faint* cry), when to use the word (formal, informal, slang, or archaic use), an example sentence or phrase showing the word in use, cross-references to other related words in the dictionary, homophones (e.g., *wrap, rap*), parts of speech, inflected endings, and explanations of how words are divided at the ends of lines.

**5.** *Understanding definitions.* The definitions are probably the most important part of the dictionary, because most people, when they think of a dictionary, think of meanings. One usually uses a dictionary to check a word's meaning, less so its spelling or pronunciation. Most words in a school dictionary have more than one meaning, so they are given more than one definition as in the example above. Each definition is numbered, and numbering either begins with the oldest definition or the most common definition. When meanings are arranged in historical order, the user can follow the growth or change in the meaning of the word. A good definition must do one or more of several things: describe the word, classify it, give examples of it, provide synonyms and contrasting words, and sometimes illustrate the word. Providing complete definitions in language that young children can understand is difficult, so definitions in a children's dictionary are not usually as robust as those found in high school, college, or general dictionaries.

**6.** *Pronunciation keys.* This part describes the clues available to pronounce an entry word. The clues are symbols of a phonetic alphabet; some are regular letters and others are special symbols. English is not a phonetic language, and many letters of the alphabet represent more than one speech sound. Consider the different sounds represented by the letter *a* in the words *gale, plan, father, above, call.* Different symbols are needed to represent the different vowel sounds. Unlike the letters of the alphabet, each pronunciation symbol represents only one sound. Pronunciation symbols are written between slant lines to distinguish them from letters. A hyphen separates the syllables, and stress marks are used to tell the student which syllable to stress in speech.

The job of using a pronunciation key is not simple, and even many adults have trouble with it. Required are translating the phonetic symbols to sounds (thus, in effect, learning an additional code), noting the separate syllables and their stress marks, and combining all this to pronounce a word—a major challenge to the average third grader. Students will need to practice using the pronunciation key with known and unknown words to become adept at its use. Pronunciation keys are reproduced at the bottom of alternative pages of the dictionary as well as in the front matter.

**7.** *Variant spellings.* This is a section that deals with words with more than one spelling (e.g., *catsup, ketchup; disk, disc; catalog, catalogue*). Dictionaries typically highlight variant spellings within the entry. Entry words are listed by the most common spelling or are listed as separate entries with both spellings and cross-references.

**8.** *Parts of speech.* This section shows the function labels for how words are used in a sentence. The function labels are abbreviations (e.g., *n., v., adj., adv., pron.*) and are presented after the entry word's pronunciation. Other function labels include prefix, suffix, and the inflected forms.

**9.** *Cross-references.* This section explains how readers are referred from one entry word to another in the dictionary. Cross-referenced words are usually synonyms (e.g., *slavery, bondage*) or examples of the entry words (e.g., *northern lights, aurora borealis*).

**10.** *Notes and explanations.* This part describes the system used by the dictionary to provide additional information about the entry word beyond what is ordinarily found in the entry. Some notes require only a few words, but others fill a paragraph. Content of the notes and explanations may vary from telling how or when a word is used, giving an example of its use, discussing the differences between certain synonyms, to relating an interesting story of the history of the word.

**11.** *Word finder table.* This is the section that explains the use of the dictionary's table of alternative spellings. Just as certain English letters represent different sounds, so, too, are the sounds of English represented by more than one spelling. This fact can cause confusion about how to spell a word and hence how to look the word up in the dictionary when the user is not certain about its spelling. Suppose a student does not know how to spell *calf.* The word finder table will show that alternative spellings of the /k/ sound at the beginning of a word are *c* and *k*. By checking these alternatives in the word finder table, the student is helped to the location of the word *calf.*

Most of the new dictionaries contain special features found on highlighted pages interspersed throughout the work. Some dictionaries contain separate tables of common abbreviations or lists of illustrations of common signs and symbols (e.g., @, %, $, &). Some of the special features to be found in student dictionaries are comprised of names and capitals of states, provinces, nations, and other geographical features; names and dates of presidents and vice-presidents; maps; information about the states including the state mottoes, flowers, and birds; and tables of weights and measures. The *Webster's New World Children's Dictionary* (Neufeldt & de Mello Vianna, 1997) has a number of extra features. Among them are boxed lists of synonyms, word histories, spelling tips, and word-building activities using prefixes and suffixes.

Dictionaries published for today's elementary and middle school students are, by and large, comprehensive, accurate, well designed, and potentially valuable to any student wanting to look up a word for information on its spelling, pronunciation, meanings, grammatical functions, or more. Nonetheless, print dictionaries come up short compared to the electronic word resources available now and described following the Teaching Suggestions.

*Teaching Suggestions*

**1.** Early in the school year it is advisable to give students a detailed "walk through" of the class dictionary and some practice with its use. The front matter pages of a good student dictionary do a commendable job of providing the required explanatory information and sometimes practice exercises. Users, of course, must know alphabetical order and how to alphabetize to the third or fourth letter. Show students how the dictionary is organized and the function of its guide words. Examine a sample entry, then check on several within the dictionary to become aware of the kinds of information available. Special attention will be required for the pronunciation key, because using the key is difficult for most elementary school students and many middle schoolers. Explore such elements as cross-referencing, special notes, and the word finder table. Visit the extra feature pages (e.g., abbreviations, states, maps, symbols), and their value will be realized by your students. Time spent learning how to use the class dictionary is student and teacher time well spent.

**2.** A major challenge to teachers is to help students develop the habit of using the dictionary as often as it is needed. One way to develop this habit is by stimulating interest in the dictionary through the use of problem-solving activities. Create problems with your class that make it necessary for them to use a dictionary. Here are some examples.

*Pretentious English.*    Students use their dictionaries to try to unravel common proverbs and other challenges such as idioms, book titles, songs, or current television shows that have been "hidden" in pretentious language:

> Everything that coruscates is not auric. (All that glitters is not gold.)
>
> Rapidity produces profligacy. (Haste makes waste.)
>
> Thorough knowledge of something or someone engenders disdain. (Familiarity breeds contempt.)
>
> All cumuli possess an argentic edging. (Every cloud has a silver lining.)

*Category Word Sort.*    Students are given a list of words and asked to put them into three categories with the help of a dictionary. For example, can they sort these words into three occupational categories?

| | |
|---|---|
| contralto | comedian |
| accountant | auditor |
| principal | lecturer |
| mime | executive |
| juggler | professor |
| proprietor | counselor |

The three categories are business, education, and entertainment. Words could be drawn from readings and coursework that is under way or will soon begin.

*Do These Words Go Together?*   Give the class a set of word pairs. The words in each pair should be difficult enough to demand the use of a dictionary. You may want students to work in small groups for this activity. They should determine whether or not the two words would likely go together, then explain why or why not.

| | |
|---|---|
| bored agog | lilting limerick |
| thrilling odyssey | apathetic enthusiast |
| loving vertigo | planned improvisation |

*What's the Answer?*   Pose questions that probably will require dictionary consultation to answer. Students, again, should be ready to talk about why they answered as they did.

1. Why would a *veterinarian* be familiar with *talons*?
2. How are a *kazoo* and a *recorder* alike?
3. Is *conquered* a synonym for *defeated*?
4. How is a *lugger* like a *kayak*?
5. Is there such a thing as a *bewildered horizon*?
6. Can you touch an *insight*?
7. What do *mauve* and *magenta* have in common?
8. Could a *gross* person be *vulgar*?
9. How could a *tornado* result in a *shambles*?
10. If you were *famished*, would you turn down a *croissant*?

Again, create your problems from words that can be found in your class dictionary and encourage class members to explain the reasons for the answers they give.

A third dictionary activity, especially for younger children, is to create a class dictionary and add new words to it regularly. Your students can become budding lexicographers. By the end of the year the class will have created a dictionary of words they know. Computers and word processors have greatly facilitated the alphabetization requirements of this type of activity for children.

## *Electronic Dictionaries*

The twenty-first century may be remembered as the golden age of electronic reference works because the 1990s saw enormous expansion in the availability, sophistication, and usefulness of such resources. As we have seen, the history of lexicography dates back to the second millennium B.C. The seventeenth century was an era of development of national and bilingual dictionaries, necessitated by the trade and missionary involvements of the time. The eighteenth century was the period of development of major diachronic (historical) dictionaries. The nineteenth century was a time of large-scale dictionary projects and the compilation of several specialized dictionaries. The twentieth century ushered in the information age and its consequent need for reference works of every type. The efforts of lexicographers toward the end of the century were greatly facilitated by computer applications that proliferated in the 1980s and 1990s. Three types of electronic dictionaries were developed and refined during these decades, and they surely will undergo dramatic improvements in the twenty-first century: CD-ROMs, reference suites, and Internet dictionaries.

Dictionaries on CD-ROMs have several notable features. Searches can be conducted from various starting points. For example, the user can type in a word and the definition appears on the screen. Or searchers can begin with the word, together with its parts of speech, its etymology, or even its pronunciation. Some CD-ROMs have anagram features that list all the words that can be formed from a single word. Some have a wild card feature that allows the user to type in a question mark when uncertain about the spelling of a word. Some will provide a list of plausible words for a word that has been misspelled when typed in. On some CD-ROMs each word is defined, pronounced, and "hot linked" to other words with connected meanings. Some have sound effects. Some provide word histories and language notes. Some include film and animation clips. *The American Heritage Talking Dictionary* (1994) includes more than 200,000 words, and it provides complete definitions, parts of speech, usage samples, hyphenation, idioms, synonyms, and abbreviations. Each word is pronounced by a trained linguist. It has a feature that allows users to locate words with just part of the definition or just part of the spelling. One CD-ROM dictionary contains 4,000 color illustrations and photographs (Sorrow & Lumpkin, 1996, p. 69). An electronic lexical database for researchers became available on CD-ROM from MIT Press. It is the *Wordnet* (Fellbaum, 1998) described in Chapter 3.

A major type of electronic reference available on store shelves in 1999 was the "reference suite." Reference suites, on CD-ROMs, included an encyclopedia, a dictionary to look up unfamiliar words in the encyclopedia, an atlas to locate places being read about, an almanac for statistics not usually found in an encyclopedia, and various other reference tools such as a thesaurus and a book of quotations. The suites were linked to the Web for updating and supplementing information. Their size, on average, was five CD-ROMs. The beauty of the suites was the integration, the linking together of the various components to make access easy. Three popular suites that were produced in 1999, the *1999 World Book Family Reference Suite, with Via*

*Voice; Encarta Reference Suite 99;* and the *1999 Grolier Multimedia Reference Suite,* consumed large amounts of memory (e.g., Encarta's five CD-ROMs use 196 megabytes). The newcomer "glitches," such as diction errors and unclear directions, will fade as the products are refined. The potential benefits of well-developed, fully integrated, multimedia reference suites hold exciting promise for the years ahead.

The Internet is the most recent electronic medium for dictionary access. Leading the way is the venerable *Oxford English Dictionary.* The second edition of *OED* became available on CD-ROM in its entirety in 1992. Hailed by *Library Journal* as "the be-all and end-all, the ultimate source . . . a finished masterpiece" (*Linguistics,* 1998–1999, p. 60), however, the *OED* is not "finished." The entire second edition was scheduled for release on the Internet in late 1999 as a searchable database—quite an accomplishment for a 20-volume, 22,000-page, 615,100-entry word dictionary. The challenge was to get all this material on-line in a way easily accessible, rapidly searchable, comfortable to read, and requiring a minimal amount of scrolling.

The third print edition of *OED* is scheduled for publication in 2010. Before that time, most of the new and revised material will become available on the Internet. The electronic format will allow frequent updates to the text more quickly, as well as powerful text searches. As the revisions progress, new entries will be added on-line quarterly, complementing but not replacing earlier ones. Each entry will contain for each word the definitions, variant spellings, etymologies, and citations of the word as it has been used in English literature. On-line users will be able to search for these elements independently (e.g., all words that entered English during the 1950s, or all words that entered English from Basque). The *OED* is one of the first Internet dictionaries to exist, but it is likely that in the twenty-first century, Internet dictionaries will abound until other newer technologies come along to make them obsolete.

## Teaching Suggestions

**1.** Help your students become familiar and comfortable with the electronic reference materials found in your school. They will need the opportunity to explore the CD-ROM dictionaries and thesauri as well as the reference suites. Some suites such as the Grolier package are geared toward younger children, but all require tryouts so that the user can become familiar with the components and how they are linked together. Even when the organization is clear and intuitive, "practice makes perfect." Once the CD-ROM dictionaries and reference suites become "old hat," your students will begin to realize their full value.

**2.** Consider devoting a class period to instruction and review of Internet vocabulary resources. An exploration of the Web site for an on-line bookstore will be an eye-opener to some of your students. Have them conduct searches at the Web site for student dictionaries, thesauri, and specialized dictionaries. From these searches, students will discover hot links or Web site addresses to dictionaries of interest to them. Visiting a dictionary Web site can be an extraordinary opportunity to learn about the art and science of lexicography as well as about individual words. The *Oxford English Dictionary* (www.oed.com), for example, highlights a new word each day and gives it full lexicographical treatment.

Individuals learn most words through oral communication and wide reading, some from direct instruction, and a great number through consulting a good dictionary or thesaurus as they seek the words, meanings, pronunciations, and spellings that they need. In a perfect world, every student in every grade in every school would have access to his or her own dictionary and thesaurus.

In the next chapter we look at the importance of the integration of the language arts and all the school subjects. We will explore the critical role that vocabulary—including vocabulary reference works—plays in supporting the interconnectedness of all the language processes, written and oral, productive and receptive.

## *References*

Berg, D. L. (1993). *A guide to the Oxford English dictionary*. Oxford, UK: Oxford University Press.

Bernstein, T. M. (1975). *Bernstein's reverse dictionary*. New York: New York Times Books.

Crystal, D. (1997). *The Cambridge encyclopedia of language* (2nd ed.). Cambridge, UK: Cambridge University Press.

Dutch, R. A. (Ed.). (1965). *The original Roget's thesaurus of English words and phrases*. New York: St. Martin's Press.

*Encarta reference suite 99* [CD-ROM]. (1999). New York: Microsoft.

*Encarta world English dictionary*. (1999). New York: St. Martin's Press and Microsoft.

Fellbaum, C. (Ed.). (1998). *Wordnet: An electronic lexical database*. Cambridge, MA: The MIT Press.

Hirsch, E. D., Jr., Kett, J. F., & Trefil, J. (1988). *The dictionary of cultural literacy*. Boston: Houghton Mifflin Company.

Kenyon, J. S., & Knott, T. A. (1953). *A pronouncing dictionary of American English*. Springfield, MA: G. & C. Merriam Company.

Klatt, E., Roy, D., Klatt, G., & Messinger, H. (Eds.). (1983). *Langenscheidts taschenwoerterbuch: English*. Berlin, Germany: Langenscheidt.

*Linguistics*. (1998–1999). Oxford, UK: Oxford University Press.

Miller, G. A. (1996). *The science of words*. New York: Scientific American Library.

Murray, J. (Ed.). (1928). *Oxford English dictionary*. Oxford, UK: Oxford University Press.

Neufeldt, V., & de Mello Vianna, F. (Eds.). (1997). *Webster's new world children's dictionary*. New York: Macmillan.

*1999 Grolier multimedia reference suite* [CD-ROM]. (1999). Chicago: Grolier Interactive.

*1999 World Book family reference suite, with via voice* [CD-ROM]. (1999). New York: I.B.M.

*The Oxford English dictionary on CD-ROM* [CD-ROM]. (1992, 1993). Oxford, UK: Oxford University Press.

Richardson, M. (1998). *Whose bright idea was that? Great firsts of world history.* New York: Kodansha International.

Simpson, J. (Ed.). (1989). *The Oxford English dictionary* (2nd ed.). Oxford, UK: Oxford University Press.

Sorrow, B. H., & Lumpkin, B. S. (1996). *CD-ROM for librarians and educators* (2nd ed.). Jefferson, NC: McFarland.

*Webster's collegiate thesaurus.* (1976). Springfield, MA: G. & C. Merriam Company.

Winchester, S. (1998). *The professor and the madman: A tale of murder, insanity, and the making of the Oxford English dictionary.* New York: HarperCollins Publishers.

Young, S. (1991). *The new comprehensive American rhyming dictionary.* New York: Avon Books.

# *Making Connections*

## *Words across the Curriculum*

*The belief that all genuine education comes about through experience
does not mean that all experiences are genuinely or equally educative.
(Dewey, 1938, p. 25)*

Even though this book has separate chapters on vocabulary and reading,
vocabulary and writing, and vocabulary and oral language, the reader is reminded that in everyday life the language arts are fully and inescapably interrelated, intertwined, and integrated. We could not sensibly pull listening,
speaking, reading, and writing apart in daily use even if we wanted to. Each
is an element in the communication process, and they are all mutually rein-
forcing. I have separated them in this book to highlight aspects of vocabulary development, understanding, and application most associated with a
particular process of language.

Just as I support integrated approaches to the language arts, so, too, do
I favor interdisciplinary teaching and learning within an integrated curriculum. In life all things are interconnected; it is primarily in schools (and uni-
versities) that we fragment the curriculum. Schools offer separate courses in
science, English, and math, separate social studies courses in history, geog-
raphy, and the other social studies disciplines, and even separate periods for
reading, language arts, and spelling. There are historical reasons for these
practices and practical realities to be considered for their continuation (e.g.,
grade-to-grade coordination, parental expectations, standardized testing).
My preference is for a curriculum that is interdisciplinary and integrated

when it makes sense to do so. Factors that contribute to "when it makes sense" include supportive administrators and parents, willing teachers, mutual planning times, compelling organizing themes, topics, or issues, and teacher recognition that skills and strategies need to be developed within the integrated projects. The integrated curriculum is more readily achieved in a self-contained elementary classroom that has one principal teacher than it is in a middle school that is partially or completely departmentalized and in which several teachers would need to be supported to work together on the integration.

In *Thought and Language* (1962), Vygotsky said, "What a child can do in cooperation today he can do alone tomorrow" (p. 104). Current pedagogical processes such as cooperative learning, group problem solving, and cross-age tutoring owe some of their heritage to research that evolved under the influence of Vygotsky. The spread of cooperative learning in the United States has been due in large part to the work of Slavin (1983) and Johnson and Johnson (1991). Not all tales of cooperative learning speak of success, though. As with so many things in life, moderate use is usually superior to too much or too little use.

Some curricula place learners in passive roles. An alternative to passivity is problem-based learning. Borich (1996) stated, "Problem-based learning organizes the curriculum around loosely structured problems that learners solve by using knowledge and skills from several disciplines" (p. 413). Students must identify needs, define pertinent words, plan and conduct research, act to resolve the problem, and reflect on the final product or solution. Interdisciplinary, integrated learning may be developed from a central theme or issue as well as from a problem (Wood, 1996).

Several decades of schema theory research have shown us that we learn best when we can relate new words and understandings to things we already know. The richer our schema, that is, the more prior knowledge we have about a topic, the more likely we are to assimilate still more. Similarly, when we are helped to make connections between seemingly disparate but actually related phenomena, our learning of the phenomena is enhanced. Interdisciplinary teaching and learning with an integrated curriculum is sound because of the many connections that exist among human knowledge.

Since the 1960s, "language across the curriculum" has been a catch-phrase heard in schools and on campuses. The person perhaps most cited for his advocacy of the concept has been Bullock (1975) who said, "Each school should have an organized policy for language across the curriculum, establishing every teacher's involvement in language and reading development throughout the years of schooling" (p. 514). His report stressed that language use in every subject was critical both for language development and for learning the concepts—the words—critical to the discipline. This contention makes common sense. To learn any subject matter, one must learn the relevant concepts, facts, skills, and processes. These are almost always expressed as or in words. Thus, learning vocabulary is essential for learning any subject. Taba (1962) stated, "It is recognized that learning is more effective when facts and principles from one field can be related to another" (p. 298). Because vocabulary study is an integral part of specific content learning, O'Rourke (1974) argued for the "integration of disciplines wherever practicable" (p. 91).

## Multiple-Meaning Words

You are reminded that English has tens of thousands of multiple-meaning words. How many meanings, for example, can you think of for the word *down?* The meanings are considerably different in *climb down the ladder, get down to work, go down to the corner store, take a statement down, pay fifty dollars down, put someone down, be down by a field goal, get a first down, wear a down coat, be down and out,* and *to hunker down.* How many meanings can you think of for these words: *drive, point, line, green, cross, stroke?* Multiple-meaning words have the potential of being especially troublesome in an integrated curriculum project, because some words represent different meanings in different disciplines. Four sets of examples are given next. As you read these lists, consider the first meaning that comes to your mind for each word and then think of the meaning that usually is associated with the word in that discipline.

|         | *Math*    |         |
|---------|-----------|---------|
| foot    | solid     | root    |
| plot    | peck      | square  |
| power   | construct | product |
| drill   | difference| yard    |
| partial | times     | mean    |
| curve   | order     | point   |

|         | *Science* |         |
|---------|-----------|---------|
| motion  | force     | fault   |
| prove   | degree    | balance |
| wave    | current   | host    |
| core    | organ     | matter  |
| crust   | cell      | rock    |
| charge  | resistance| funnel  |

|         | *Social Studies* |         |
|---------|------------------|---------|
| key     | bill             | product |
| race    | plain            | group   |
| ruler   | market           | range   |
| country | crop             | cabinet |

| state | land | bay |
|-------|------|-----|
| legend | run | value |

*English*

| case | number | tragedy |
|------|--------|---------|
| mood | tense | article |
| appendix | subject | tone |
| dash | voice | pitch |
| diagram | juncture | romance |
| person | act | stress |

Experienced teachers help their students develop a mindset for diversity—an expectation that any new word they encounter probably has more than one meaning, and that it is the student's job to determine which meaning fits the context. Words in specific disciplines frequently take on new meanings as shown in the lists above. Consider the dilemma a student faces when confronting square roots in math, tree roots in science, the roots of words in English, and the roots of families in social studies. Teachers who involve their students in interdisciplinary integrated units of study bear special responsibility for helping students learn the context-appropriate meanings.

## Integrated Curriculum Units

Two types of interdisciplinary, integrated thematic units are described in this chapter: out-of-the-ordinary units and community construction projects. "Out-of-the-ordinary" is not used here to mean unusual, extraordinary, strange, or weird, but rather it means a theme based on ordinary, common, everyday, taken-for-granted objects or ideas. As long ago as pre–World War II, the importance of organizing instruction around everyday experiences was touted by John Dewey (1938) who said:

> One consideration stands out clearly when education is conceived in terms of experience. Anything which can be called a study, whether arithmetic, history, geography, or one of the natural sciences must be derived from materials which at the outset fall within the scope of ordinary life-experiences. In this respect the newer education contrasts sharply with procedures which start with facts and truths that are outside the range of experience of those taught. (p. 73)

Thirty or more years of research have confirmed that we learn best when we can relate new knowledge to prior knowledge (*What Works*, 1987, p. 55).

Integrated out-of-the-ordinary units begin with a central topic that students explore using two or more of the disciplines. The usual sequence of events includes selecting a unit theme, creating a word web, using and defining important vocabulary, planning and conducting research, preparing presentation materials, sharing results, and comparing and reflecting on findings. These steps are exemplified in the following discussion of a unit on *shoes*.

### Teaching Suggestion

*Out-of-the-Ordinary Unit on* **shoes.** The purpose of the unit is to integrate several disciplines including social studies, language arts, science, and math through studying a common, everyday item—the shoe. Another purpose is to help students hone their research skills.

Did you know that each foot has 26 bones, 19 muscles, 4 arches, 107 ligaments, a mile of blood vessels and nerves, and hundreds of thousands of sweat glands and pores? That the big toe has two bones but the other toes each have three? That the average person takes 2,000 steps a day and the feet absorb 500 tons of pressure daily? That the average person walks the equivalent of four-and-one-half times around the globe in a lifetime (Bata's *All About Shoes*, 1994, p. 61)? These and many other facts, stories, anecdotes, artworks, songs, and historical and cultural insights about shoes were discovered during an out-of-the-ordinary unit on *shoes*. The unit was undertaken by elementary education majors in my integrated language-arts/social-studies methods class. Other findings included:

- One cowhide yields about 16 pairs of shoes, 18 soccer balls, or 144 baseballs.
- Spanish cave paintings depicting men and women wearing boots of animal skins and fur were created about 13,000 B.C. Egyptian sandals were believed to be first worn in about 3,500 B.C.
- Before King George IV, shoes were not shaped and could be worn on either foot.
- Shoestrings were invented in 1790. Before then, buckles were used on shoes.
- Travelers in the seventeenth century used the hollow heels of shoes to hide valuables from highway robbers.
- The zipper was used in galoshes (1873) before it was used in clothing.
- More than 100 operations go into constructing a shoe.
- The first high heels were worn by Egyptian butchers.
- The most famous pair of shoes in the world probably is the sparkling ruby slippers Judy Garland wears in the movie *The Wizard of Oz*.

*Selecting a Unit Theme.* There is no shortage of out-of-the-ordinary topics around which to organize an integrated unit. Virtually anything is fair game—any everyday object, topic, issue, problem, or experience. Sometimes the unit theme is chosen by the school curriculum, other times by the grade level team or by the teacher, and in some cases by the class. The following is a representative list to help you realize the almost unlimited variety of possible topics. In the list, each general category is followed by just three specific examples.

**CLOTHING:** shoes, uniforms, hats
**FOOD:** pasta, cheese, cookies
**HOBBIES:** stamps, fishing, music
**SPORTS:** powerlifting, jogging, basketball
**FINE ARTS:** sculpture, dance, painting
**FEELINGS:** joy, fear, relief
**SOCIETAL ISSUES:** homelessness, terrorism, human rights
**CURRENT PROBLEMS:** inflation, unemployment, health
**FARM PRODUCTS:** rice, pecans, sugar
**POLICE WORK:** fingerprints, voice prints, bugs
**MUSIC:** reggae, Cajun, blues
**TRANSPORTATION:** ferry boats, walking, subways
**YOUTH ISSUES:** homework, rules, rivalries
**ANIMALS:** camels, alligators, armadillos
**MACHINES:** blender, gumball, elevator

The list could go on. Any ordinary event, issue, object, feeling, or belief can become the central focus of an integrated, interdisciplinary unit of study. The unit exemplified in the following pages had *shoes* as its theme.

*Creating a Word Web.* Word webs are graphic organizers that illustrate lists of related words associated with a central concept (see Chapter 3 for a detailed discussion). There are different ways that words may relate to the central concept. These include but are not restricted to examples of the concept, synonyms, types, uses, functions, and features. Word webs are created by the whole class as directed by the teacher. The following is the typical sequence of steps in the webbing process.

**1.** The teacher writes the central concept on a transparency or the chalkboard (e.g., the unit theme *shoes*).

**2.** Several category labels are placed on the web by the teacher (e.g., purposes, kinds, parts).

**3.** One or two examples are written below two or three of the category labels (e.g., purposes: protection, comfort, beauty).

**4.** After discussing the words on this starter web, class members are asked to independently consider what they know about shoes and then on a sheet of paper to copy the starter map and add any new words or new categories they can recall.

**5.** Next, the students are engaged in a full-class, brainstorming session. Based on their personal reflections, they can recommend new words and categories to be added to the starter web used by the teacher.

**6.** Finally, and most important, the teacher leads the students in a discussion of the words on the web. The goal is to "tease out" similarities and differences in the words. The students are asked to discuss their own experiences with some of the words. Volunteers are asked to use words in sentences. This period of discussion helps get the integrated unit off to a strong start.

Figure 6.1 presents a starter web for the *shoe* unit under discussion. Word webbing leads to learning new words in ways that mirror how we organize words in our mental lexicons in fields of semantically related concepts. Webbing helps students access their prior knowledge, modify it, and, of course, add to it.

***Defining Important Vocabulary.*** Students will learn new words at all stages in the integrated unit, beginning with the word web kick-off, continuing into the unit planning and research, and on through the research presentations and the end-of-unit discussions. Some of the words will have more than one meaning that will be new and unexpected to the students.

Some teachers have students keep a vocabulary journal in which they add new words and new meanings as they learn them. Synonyms,

**FIGURE 6.1** *Starter Word Web for* **shoes.**

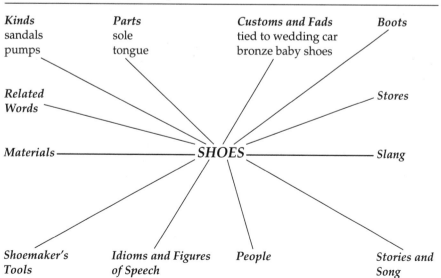

examples, and short definitions are included together with sample sentences from unit materials or those written by the students. Other teachers have the class compile an all-class vocabulary notebook that increasingly can serve as both a class dictionary and thesaurus for the unit. The sheer quantity of new vocabulary learned during an integrated unit surprises both students and teachers. The benefit is that the words are learned in relation to a well-known concept (e.g., *shoes*). The following lists contain words, expressions, and facts compiled in my methods class notebook developed throughout our *shoe* unit.

### Purposes of Shoes

| | |
|---|---|
| protect the feet | beauty and fashion |
| religious practice | sports performance |
| power and authority | status symbols |
| work performance | dance performance |
| comfort | health and anatomy |

### Kinds of Shoes

| | | |
|---|---|---|
| sandals | clown | slingback wedges |
| slippers | mules | costume |
| moccasins | loafers | top siders |
| espadrilles | platforms | oxfords |
| tap dance | brogans | saddle |
| high heels | spikes | super spikes |
| pumps | ballet | driving |
| tree climbing | wing tips | rice field |
| flats | billboards | chestnut crushers |
| elevated | lumberjack | sheep shearing |
| peat bog clogs | steel toed | sacrificial |
| wooden | funeral | tennis |

### Kinds of Boots

| | | |
|---|---|---|
| bicycle | duck | half |
| eel | ice skates | thigh-highs |
| mosquito | roller skates | race car |
| moon | hiking | pant |
| armored | sprinting | sock |
| deep sea | mountaineering | walking |
| space | afternoon | cut-outs |
| prison | flower-power | cowboy/cowgirl |
| hunting | galoshes | overshoes |
| nobleperson | Wellingtons | military |
| button | zipper | hook-and-eye |

### What Shoes Are Made Of

| | | |
|---|---|---|
| leather | satin | plastic |
| fur | velvet | suede |
| canvas | straw | cork |
| rubber | feathers | beads |
| brocade | wood | paper |

### Parts of a Shoe

| | | |
|---|---|---|
| heel | welt | quarter lining |
| top lift | toe cap | hooks and eyes |
| shank | throat | counter |
| sole | vamp | quarter |
| insole | tongue | buckles |
| laces | straps | buttons |
| Velcro tabs | zippers | decorations |

### Shoemaker's Tools

| | | |
|---|---|---|
| last | awl | glazing heel iron |
| edge setter | rasp | welt cutter |
| hammer | nipper | moon knife |
| scissors | stitcher | hand protector |

### Slang for Shoes and Feet

| | | |
|---|---|---|
| boats | jellies | gunboats |
| kicks | sneaks | clodhoppers |
| sneakers | stumpers | hocks |
| dogs | pins | barking dogs |

### Idioms and Figures of Speech

| | |
|---|---|
| comfortable as an old shoe | drop the other shoe |
| put the shoe on the other foot | if the shoe fits, wear it |
| be in someone else's shoes | starting on a shoestring |
| give someone the boot | boot someone out |
| shake in one's boots | cool your heels |
| you bet your boots | boot hill |
| boot camp | bootlegger |
| bootlicker | one foot in the grave |
| footloose and fancy free | foot the bill |
| get off on the wrong foot | get one's foot in the door |
| hot foot it out of here | not set foot somewhere |
| put one's best foot forward | put one's foot down |
| wait on someone hand and foot | play footsie |
| foot-in-mouth disease | at one's feet |

off one's feet

on one's feet

get your feet wet

stand on your own two feet

back on one's feet

follow in someone's footsteps

get cold feet

jump in with both feet

kick up your heels

thinking on your feet

head over heels

shoestring budget

### Shoes in Story and Song

Wizard of Oz

Cinderella

The Elves and the Shoemaker

The Red Shoes

Alligator Shoes

My Best Shoes

Shoes Like Miss Alice's

Shoes, Shoes, Shoes

Whose Shoes?

Armadillo Rodeo

Not So Fast, Songololo

Olive Button Is a Sissy

Blue Suede Shoes

These Boots Were Made for Walkin'

There Was an Old Woman . . .

### Shoe Customs and Fads

throw shoes at the bride

bronze baby shoes

wear unlaced tennies

wear beads on safety pins

tie shoes to newlyweds' car

collect miniature shoes

### Related Words

| | | |
|---|---|---|
| shoebox | shoelace | shoemaker |
| shoeblack | shoeshine | shoespoon |
| shoehorn | shoestring | shoe tree |
| shoelace | football | foot locker |
| foot bath | footfall | foothill |
| foothold | footloose | footnote |
| footpath | footprint | footrest |
| footstep | footwear | arch support |

Most of the new words in the unit are learned through concept associations with similar but somewhat different words (e.g., How is a moccasin like a loafer but different?). Others are learned through contexts encountered while doing research (e.g., "The steel soles and heels on her tap dance shoes could be heard a block away"). Sometimes dictionaries and thesauri, both print and electronic, are checked to pin down the precise meanings of words and expressions. Some encyclopedias and reference sites on CD-ROMs hold a wealth of information.

Recall the discussion in Chapter 1 that slang expressions and idioms are lexical items that need to be learned in the same ways as individual words. This is because their meanings are not dependent on the meanings of the separate words within them. Tracking the origins of some of the expressions can require serious research, even though their meanings often can be determined through context and good inferential logic.

*Planning and Conducting Research.*   The class should be divided into teams to undertake the research. Usually each team is asked to begin by listing some questions of interest to them that can serve to guide their research. The following are sample research planning questions from the *shoe* unit.

### Who

What type of person wore this kind of shoe?

Were they worn by young or senior persons?

Was this shoe worn by men or women?

Would the owners of such a shoe most likely be rich or poor?

### What

What is the shoe made of?

What would it feel like to wear it?

What was the cost of such a shoe?

What was its main function?

What other types of clothing would be worn with the shoe?

What kind of noise would the shoe make?

What do signs of wear and damage tell about a shoe and the person who wore it?

### When

When was this type of shoe worn?

Does the shoe resemble footwear from other periods?

Can the shoe be compared to anything worn today?

Was this shoe worn daily or only for a certain purpose or on a special occasion?

### Where

What was the climate like where this shoe was worn?

Was the shoe worn indoors, outdoors, or both?

What country or region is this shoe from?

*Why*

Why is this shoe shaped the way it is?

Why is the shoe decorated as it is?

Why is the shoe made from these materials and not others?

Why was this type of shoe worn as opposed to others?

*How*

How was this shoe made, by hand or by machine?

How did the shoe influence the way a person walked, moved, or stood?

How was the shoe put on and taken off?

How much would the shoe weigh?

How comfortable would the shoe have been to wear?

Teams may direct their research efforts toward specific entries on the initiating word web, in addition to answering the questions. Intriguing anecdotes are bound to surface.

To conduct the research, the team decides who is going to look into what, sets deadlines, and decides how to organize the information team members acquire. Then the research gets under way and each member carries out his or her agreed upon tasks. Student research will lead them to books, articles, and CD-ROMs. They will search the World Wide Web using such search engines as Alta Vista and Yahoo! to locate helpful Web sites. Some students may visit local retailers, dealers, producers, designers, or malls. Others will write letters to public agencies, corporations, and manufacturers. Experts can be contacted or, if local, visited. Team members are responsible for organizing the information they collect.

*Planning Presentation Materials and Sharing Results.*    Each team is charged with presenting its research findings, conclusions, and observations to the entire class. The teams must plan what they will present and how they will present it. Presentation formats could include panel discussions, audio- or videotaped interviews, skits or dramatizations, graphic organizers such as time lines, maps, comparison tables, or word webs. Other presentations might include electronically assisted demonstrations, "talk show" formats, Socratic dialogues, posters and murals, taped or live "commercials," songs, case studies, "taste tests," prediction quizzes, contests, and, of course, oral reports with handouts.

Teams will need to be informed of their allotted presentation times, and a presentation schedule should be posted in the classroom. Remind students to make their presentations informative, lively, and engaging.

*Comparing and Reflecting on Findings.* After all teams have made their presentations, the teacher needs to conduct a class discussion intended to generate reflections, comparisons, and conclusions about the out-of-the-ordinary theme and all else that has been learned. This gives students the opportunity to see similarities and differences between team findings, note unexpected commonalities, and perhaps learn some of life's lessons. You can help your students be aware of how the different disciplines have come into play during the unit. You can help them elaborate, extend, diverge, and form generalizations. You can help them see that "free" materials sent by manufacturers or organizations are often colorful, glitzy, and persuasive—informative but not unbiased. You can help your students develop historical, cultural, economic, and aesthetic perspectives on ordinary, everyday things.

In summary, the objectives accomplished by this unit were having students:

- Engage in advance planning through the use of word webs
- Learn the meanings and uses of related words
- Plan and conduct research
- Compare and reflect on results

In the process of meeting these objectives, students learned some science, math, social studies, and more about their language.

Through participation in interdisciplinary, integrated thematic units about out-of-the-ordinary topics, students come to understand the interrelatedness of all things, and they make the connections that help them make sense of their world. They learn new words and new meanings for known words. Typically, their innate quest for learning and learning how to learn is both satisfied and stimulated.

## Teaching Suggestion

*Community Construction Project.* The major goal of a community construction project is to engage students in active, hands-on problem solving that results in a tangible, educational creation. A scale model community made mainly from recyclable materials—previously discarded junk—will be the end product. Construction projects show students the importance of planning, cooperation, and compromise to the successful completion of a major undertaking. What can your class construct? It all depends on the imagination of you and your students. The usual steps in such a project include deciding the community to construct, forming construction teams, conducting research, identifying and collecting materials, constructing components, assembling the community, and preparing promotional materials.

The community construction project described in this section was conducted by a class of fifth-grade students in a public school.

*Choosing a Community to Construct.*   The teacher explains to the students that they will be starting a project in which the whole class will create a model of a community out of recyclable materials. It will be laid out on a flat piece of cardboard or similar material about the size of a ping pong table or two, depending on the availability of space in your school. A flattened mattress box or refrigerator box or two works well for this. Have the class think about and brainstorm what kind of a community they would like to construct. The group of fifth graders came up with this list of possible communities:

| | |
|---|---|
| their city | a mountain village |
| a city of the future | a desert town |
| an imaginary city | an island community |
| a city in the past | Venice, Italy |
| a theme park | an airport |
| a farm community | a college |
| a medieval castle | a sports complex |
| a colonial village | a small town |
| a campground | an Old West town |

After animated discussion and several votes, the class decided to construct an Old West town.

*Forming Construction Teams.*   First a mayor (or leader by some title) needs to be appointed or elected and a town name chosen (e.g., *Lone Star*). The mayor then leads a discussion about the planning and construction teams that must be formed. The teams that usually are necessary to complete a community construction are:

1. landscape, which is in charge of creating landforms, vegetation, or bodies of water;
2. transportation, which is in charge of building roads, bridges, railways;
3. government, which is in charge of building schools, libraries, town halls, fire and police departments;
4. residential, which is in charge of building houses and other residential units;
5. commercial, which is in charge of building stores, banks, hotels, and other businesses; and
6. recreational, which is in charge of building parks and sports facilities.

More or fewer teams may be decided on depending on what type of community is to be constructed. Students may be allowed to volunteer for the team they want to work with, but each team should have no more than five members.

The team meets and selects a representative to the town council. The town council's jobs include developing a layout plan for the community based on the recommendations from each team, deciding on approximate sizes of buildings, determining locations of roads, and more. It settles disputes among teams (e.g., the fifth-grade commercial team designed a hotel that was too big in comparison to the government buildings; a small lake was planned for the same location as the stables). Each town council representative serves as chairperson of his or her construction team.

*Conducting Research.*     Each team engages in research needed to help them plan and construct their components for the community. Questions typical of those that must be answered are:

> What is the specific time period?
> What were the times like in, for example, the Old West?
> What did the buildings look like?
> Were there post offices, sidewalks, electricity?
> What kinds of stores and businesses were around then?
> Were there any recreational facilities?
> What did children do for fun?
> Were there lakes?
> Were most built on rivers?
> Where did people live?
> When did railroads span the country?
> How long were stagecoaches in use?
> Were there churches?

The school and community libraries, the Internet, and local experts will become valuable resources to the young researchers.

After the research is complete, the layout plan of the town may need to be modified by the town council and then superimposed on the cardboard base. Later the landscape, transportation, and recreation teams will sketch and construct where roads, shrubbery, and the like will be placed. Each construction team will need to know what space they have to work with and what size to make their buildings.

*Identifying and Collecting Materials.*     Based on both prior knowledge and research, each team plans what they will construct and what materials will be needed for construction. Tentative lists of materials need to be made and might include such items as cereal boxes, pine cones, pencil shavings, processed cheese boxes, coffee grounds, dryer lint, film canisters, paper towel rolls, used craft sticks, wire, grass, coffee cans, oatmeal cylinders, and others. When given the chance, most children show their creativity. Plastic film containers may become rain barrels, table bases, or horse bodies. Dryer lint may become steam from an engine, snow, or Spanish moss.

At the conclusion of preparing their lists, teams should inform one another of the things they need so that all class members can help one another find materials. The community construction is a full-class project involving everyone. There will need to be scissors, staplers, glue, pliers, paint brushes, and the like, available during the actual construction.

*Constructing the Components and Assembling the Community.*   Constructing and decorating the components may require several hours depending on the age and capabilities of your students. While some teams are constructing general stores, train depots, houses, and schools, other teams will be busy making and placing lakes and streams, distant mountains, sagebrush, roads, railroad tracks, parks, and more. Any disputes that arise about space allocations or other matters are to be settled by the town council. Assembling the pieces on the layout plan (which needs to be glued or in some way securely affixed to the cardboard base) largely will be done by members of the town council with assistance from team members as needed.

Gradually the community will begin to take shape. As the pieces are touched up and the community is "perfected," the students will feel a surge of pride and ownership.

*Preparing Promotional Materials.*   When not participating in the assembly of the community, students can begin work on ideas for tourist brochures and other promotional and descriptive materials. The students who worked on *Lone Star* created wagon signs (precursors to bumper stickers), postcards, business cards, and a twelve-page illustrated, duplicated tourist brochure. The tourist brochure presented a history of *Lone Star*, directions to *Lone Star*, a schedule for the *Lone Star Express* (a train), a description of the scenery (e.g., "*Lone Star* sits in the beautiful Sunset Valley. The majestic Soaring Star river flows through the heart . . ."), recreational opportunities (fishing, swimming, archery), short descriptions of every commercial and public building in *Lone Star* (general store, dress shop, jail, school, saloon, post office, stables, Wells Fargo, boarding house, etc.), and a centerfold detailed town map.

Writing promotional materials gives students authentic practice with vocabulary selection, writing, advertising, and illustrating. Research skills and habits are honed and the various disciplines are tapped.

A community construction project helps students learn that in any co-operative venture, give and take are essential. As a teacher participating in such a project, you will be aware of your natural "teacher tendency" to be prescriptive about desired outcomes and the pathways to those outcomes. My simplest advice is to get the students started and then get out of the way. Some teams will take longer to begin the task, or to jell, others may flounder a time or two, but soon most will discover their own resourcefulness. Integration will occur naturally and new vocabulary will be learned as students do the research and work cooperatively to solve the many problems associated with constructing a scale-model community from scratch.

If you can find ways to have your students work in either out-of-the-ordinary units or community construction projects, you will be helping them make connections. Those connections include connecting new vocabulary and new knowledge with known words and prior knowledge, making connections between the various disciplines, establishing connections with their teammates and classmates, and developing connections between inquiry, reflection, problem solving, and insight. Throughout the experience, you will be helping your students learn new words within the context of the curriculum rather than learning words in isolation.

## References

Bata Shoe Organization. (1994). *All about shoes: Footwear through the ages.* Toronto: Bata Limited.

Borich, G. D. (1996). *Effective teaching methods* (3rd ed.). Englewood Cliffs, NJ: Prentice-Hall.

Bullock, A. (1975). *A language for life.* London: Department of Education and Science, HMOS.

Dewey, J. (1933). *How we think* (2nd ed.). Boston: Heath.

Dewey, J. (1938). *Experience and Education.* New York: Collier Books.

Johnson, D., & Johnson, R. (1991). *Learning together and alone* (3rd ed.). Englewood Cliffs, NJ: Prentice-Hall.

Kellough, R. D., Jarolimek, J., Parker, W., Martorella, P. H., Tompkins, G. E., & Hoskisson, K. (1996). *Integrating language arts and social studies for intermediate and middle school students.* Englewood Cliffs, NJ: Merrill.

O'Rourke, J. P. (1974). *Toward a science of vocabulary development.* The Hague: Mouton.

Post, R., Ellis, A. K., Humphreys, A. H., & Buggey, L. J. (1997). *Interdisciplinary approaches to curriculum: Themes for teaching.* Upper Saddle River, NJ: Merrill.

Slavin, R. E. (1983). *Cooperative learning.* New York: Longman.

Taba, H. (1962). *Curriculum development.* New York: Harcourt Brace and World, Inc.

U.S. Department of Education. (1987). *What works: Research about teaching and learning* (2nd ed.). Washington, D.C.: Author.

Vygotsky, L. S. (1962). *Thought and language.* Cambridge, MA: MIT Press.

Wolfinger, D. M., & Stockard, J. W., Jr. (1997). *Elementary methods: An integrated curriculum.* New York: Addison Wesley Longman.

Wood, K. E. (1997). *Interdisciplinary instruction.* Upper Saddle River, NJ: Prentice-Hall.

# 7

## *The Assessment of Vocabulary*

*At present, no matter how poor a test may be, if it is nicely packaged and it promises to do all sorts of things which no test can do, the test will find many gullible buyers. . . . The well-informed test user cannot do this; he knows that the best of our tests are still highly fallible instruments which are extremely difficult to interpret with assurance in individual cases. (Buros, 1978)*

Tests, presumably, are given because they provide information to someone who needs it. Teachers give tests, observe their students, and ask questions in order to learn what their students need help with. Sometimes tests are given to evaluate instructional programs, innovations, or projects. If, for example, a teacher tries an experimental program to improve children's use of analogy strategies, pupils might be tested to see if the program worked. Large-scale, standardized assessments are conducted by school districts, states, and the federal government. Their purpose, ostensibly, is to gather data on which states, districts, or schools are performing well or poorly so that resources can be allocated accordingly. Logically, those schools or districts or states doing less well would be targeted for help in the form of more or better teachers or specialists, additional monies for instructional materials and resources, professional development for faculties, or more classrooms so class sizes can be reduced.

How much of this happens? In how many instances are important instructional or resource allocation decisions made on the basis of the testing

data? What happens after the comparisons have been made that allow some
to feel smug and others embarrassed? Do we spend too much school time
testing, assessing, measuring, probing, watching—at the expense of teaching? How many hours per week, semester, school year, does a child spend
being tested, diagnosed, or observed? To what end?

## *Problems in Assessing Vocabulary*

Assessing vocabulary knowledge is fraught with problems. The first is deciding which words to test. Where are the test words to come from? One
source of words to test could include words from a selection in one of the
subjects you teach. These words would be ones you or someone has determined to be critical to understanding the selection. Another source could be
a list of words considered to be of high frequency on some word count.
Words also could come from spelling or writing, or from a state list, or could
be the words the child wants to learn. Words with particular patterns or
morphological structures or words from various disciplines could be selected. With more than two million words in the English lexicon, there are
plenty to choose from when deciding what to test.

A second problem concerns what it means to know a word. Does
knowing a word mean being able to pronounce it when seeing it in print?
Does it mean recognizing a printed word when you hear it spoken? Both of
these are common procedures for testing sight word vocabulary. Does
knowing a word mean being able to tell its definition? If so, which definition? Most words have two or more meanings, but some words have hundreds of meanings. Does knowing a word mean being able to use it
appropriately? Orally or in writing? Does knowing a word mean being able
to tell its semantic features, to provide examples of it, to name the functions
of it, or to cite related words? Does knowing a word mean that you are able
to do all of these things with the word?

A final problem has to do with how you actually test the word. Once
you have decided what words you want to test, and what procedures will
satisfy you that they measure word knowledge, you need to consider how
best to test. Will you require students to write dictionary-type definitions of
the words even though Aitchison (1994) and Miller (1996) have reminded us
that writing definitions is a highly sophisticated lexicographical skill? Will
you have children choose, write, or orally give synonyms or antonyms? Will
you have them choose, write, or orally give examples of the word, parts of
the word, functions of the word, or use the word to complete analogies? Will
you have the students pronounce or write the word, use the word to fill in a
blank in a spoken or written sentence, or create an oral or written sentence
with the word in it? Will you have them demonstrate, dramatize, or draw an
illustration of the word? Will you test the words all of those ways? Every

type of test format will yield somewhat different information, and a student could demonstrate knowledge of a word when tested one way, but ignorance of the word when tested with another format.

In order to test word knowledge, we can ask a child to:

1. Read the word and circle a picture of it.
2. Look at a picture and circle the word for it.
3. Read the word and circle a definition.
4. Read the word and circle a synonym.
5. Read the word and circle an antonym.
6. Read the word in context and circle a definition, synonym, or antonym.
7. Read a sentence and write the missing word.
8. Read a sentence and supply the missing word orally.
9. Read the word and draw a picture or tell about it.
10. Read the word and put it in a category.
11. Find the word in a category in which it does not belong.
12. Many others.

If the target word is *elephant,* for example, it seems that a child could convincingly demonstrate a knowledge of the word *elephant* with some of the above tasks, but reveal an ignorance of the word with some of the other tasks. In a study examining vocabulary test format effects with more than eight hundred elementary school children, Johnson et al. (1978) found significant differences between three vocabulary test formats (synonym, synonym in context, cloze blank in context) constructed to measure knowledge of the same words. In other words, children "knew" a word when tested one way, but didn't "know" the same word when tested another way.

## Why Testing Has Become Important

Every state but one now has some type of required testing program in place. The tests are intended to make public schools accountable to the public. In these states, students at certain grade levels in elementary, middle, and secondary schools are required to take performance tests, at least in reading and math. Some states use state-developed tests, others use published standardized tests, and some states utilize a combination of both. Based on state performance on these tests, schools are rated and ranked, and these results typically are published in regional and state newspapers as well as on Web sites. In Louisiana, for example, each school receives a score between 0 and 200. Sixty percent of its score is based on the state-developed Louisiana Education Assessment Program (LEAP) test, 30 percent is based on a national standardized test (Iowa Test of Basic Skills), and 10 percent is based on school attendance and retention.

The Louisiana Assessment results are reported in six brackets:

| | |
|---|---|
| Schools of Academic Excellence | (150+) |
| Schools of Academic Distinction | (125–149.9) |
| Schools of Academic Achievement | (100–124.9) |
| Academically Above Average | (69.4–100) |
| Academically Below Average | (30.1–69.3) |
| Academically Unacceptable | (0–30.0) |

The assessment is considered "high stakes" because poorly performing schools that do not improve after two years could be "reconstituted"; that is, the principal and faculty could be replaced. The two types of high stakes tests are usually criterion-referenced tests that measure whether the students meet some predetermined standard (e.g., Louisiana's LEAP test) and norm-referenced tests that compare performance with the scores of other students in a national sample (e.g., Iowa Test of Basic Skills).

## Five Measurement Problems

When selecting or using published-standardized or criterion-referenced tests, teachers should read carefully the technical data in the manuals, particularly the information about validity, reliability, and the norming-population samples. Teachers need to be alert to such problems as the following:

1. *Objectivity.* A test is objective if everyone takes it under similar conditions and if it is scored in the same way for each student. Essay exams are subjective tests because the interpretation of the answers and the value given to them are dependent on the criteria of the grader. Multiple-choice tests, on the other hand, are considered objective because there is presumably one correct (and predetermined) answer to each question. Thus, with no room for subjective interpretation, it is an objective, dispassionate test—despite the fact that the test items may be ambiguous, inane, or even erroneous. For example:

Which of the following is a measure of hue?

a. 2 rods
b. 5 gallons
c. 6 pounds
d. 4 inches

The test question is gibberish—but it is technically objective.

Test objectivity should not be equated with fairness. A test (with sensible items, unlike the one above) may be objective yet discriminate against groups or individuals whose language, dialect, experience, or creative thinking is different from that of others.

**2.** *Standardization and norming.* It must be made clear that standardization, like objectivity, has no bearing on the quality of a test; it relates only to the reporting of scores. A norming sample is selected (hopefully one representative of the target users of the test), their scores are translated into grade-level equivalents or percentiles, for example, and these scores become the standard against which future test takers are judged or to which they are compared. Thus, the norming sample becomes very important. Are the norming students cross-sectionally representative of the geographical regions, community sizes, cultural and ethnic groups, grade, sex, and linguistic diversity of American school children?

**3.** *Reliability.* Reliability means how well a test agrees with itself, and how consistently it will yield the same results for the same child. If a child takes a test on Monday and again on Friday, it would be hoped that the child's score would be about the same each time. If the test is consistently, reliably measuring the same trait, the score should be similar. If the score deviates significantly, the test is probably less reliable or even unreliable.

Reliability is usually determined and a reliability coefficient (ranging from 0.00 to 1.00) obtained through one of four procedures. Test-retest reliability involves giving the test today and again at a later time and comparing the scores from the two test sessions. Parallel-form reliability involves constructing two forms of the same test to be as alike as possible, administering both forms to the same people and comparing their scores on the two forms. If the scores are quite close, reliability has been shown. Split-half reliability is sometimes done to save time. The test is administered once, and students' scores on half the test (say the even-numbered items—2, 4, 6, etc.) are compared with their scores on the other half (odd-numbered items). The closer the match, the higher the reliability. Internal consistency reliability involves a statistical procedure for determining the extent to which all items on the test measure the same abilities.

A highly reliable test—one that yields the same results for a group rather consistently—may in no way relate to the stated purpose of the test (validity is discussed next).

**4.** *Validity.* Validity is the heart of the test. Test purchasers rightly assume that the tests provided for measuring attainment of objectives are valid indices of the skills at issue. However, if a test uses paper-and-pencil measures of a non-paper-and-pencil task, then it ought, at the very least, to validate those measures by administering group and individual tests to a small sample of students. In one test, comprehension is measured by requiring the child to read silently along a passage while a teacher reads it orally. How do we ever know what is being measured with such a task? Is it listening? Reading? Both?

There are other minor validity issues, most often peculiar to specific tests. For example, test labeling appears to be a problem in one diagnostic test where the root word test really measures knowledge of prefixes, suffixes, and inflections (the distractors all have the root in common, only the affixes vary across distractors).

To make a decision based on a test score one has the right to assume that the score means something. In essence, content validity rests on the soundness of judgments of some experts who have been asked to judge whether the item measures what it says it does. Both concurrent and predictive validity rest on the assumption that the test to which the present test is being compared is itself valid.

Validation of a test seems to be a very uncertain albeit crucial business. I hope you will always ask the question when examining tests, "Does the test really measure what it says it does?"

**5.** *Other trouble spots.* Other potential weaknesses of tests include: (a) their dependence on language development; (b) their often inappropriate or outdated content; (c) their frequent incorrectness in designating a particular answer "correct" when another one of two could be just as "correct"; (d) the ambiguity of some of their directions and items; (e) their inability to provide for partial understanding (it's either right or wrong); (f) their cultural and linguistic bias toward the dominant middle class; and (g) the case of most standardized achievement tests, their lack of diagnostic value.

In short, few tests, if any, are perfect. Most test authors and publishers are in no sense charlatans. Most strive hard to be extremely careful in the construction, validation, and standardization of their tests. Most do try to account for some of the concerns mentioned here. But the net result is that some tests are much better than others. Some tests do measure what they say they do, and do it well, thus permitting their users to make informed and appropriate decisions.

## Standardized Vocabulary Tests

Most standardized reading tests include subtests of vocabulary and comprehension. The total reading score is usually a composite of the two. Typical formats for testing vocabulary on such standardized instruments include:

1. Given a list of three or four words, indicate the one that doesn't belong (e.g., carrot, beet, potato, *apple*).
2. Choose the word that fits best in the sentence (e.g., The politician _____ the voters to vote for her: *implored,* winked, dropped, refused).
3. Given a list of three or four words, choose the word closest in meaning (e.g., Students are not allowed to run in the *corridor:* staircase, playground, *hallway,* cafeteria).

Other formats in use require students to provide a word to complete an analogy, prove or select an antonym, or put words in the right categories.

If you teach in a district that administers standardized vocabulary tests or subtests, be skeptical of the results. Ask yourself these questions:

1. Where did the test words come from?
2. Why were these words selected and not others?
3. What assumptions did the test author seem to have about what it means to know a word?
4. What test format was used? Why this format and not others?
5. What do these results really mean?

How can a teacher help students prepare for such tests? Short of teaching the actual words on the test (If you did that, what would you be testing?), teachers can provide practice with the common vocabulary test formats. They can stress vocabulary development and provide continual opportunities for vocabulary growth in both oral and written language. They can engage their students often in language play activities. They can teach their pupils to use a variety of vocabulary resource works such as dictionaries and thesauri. They can encourage wide reading of all types of written materials including children's books, textbooks, magazine articles, newspapers, and documents.

## Classroom Vocabulary Tests

Assessment is a critical part of teaching. Teachers need to know the kinds of ways they can be of help to their students. They need to know if the students have learned what was taught. Standardized tests usually won't help the teacher make instructional decisions, but informal vocabulary measures can yield important information. The following are some ways in which teachers assess word knowledge in their classrooms.

**1.** *Written work.* Assign specific words the students have been taught or have been reading to be used in an assigned piece of written fiction or non-fiction. In this way you can see who is using the words correctly. Which words do they all misuse? These words should be retaught.

**2.** *Cloze passages.* Give students passages from a selection in which key words have been omitted and replaced with a blank line. See if students can supply the missing words either from choices given or from memory.

**3.** *Hinky Pinkies.* Use hinky-pinky formats and other riddles to determine specific word understanding (e.g., What would you call an English pastry food in the bell of a band instrument? A trumpet crumpet).

**4.** *Memory games.* Have students match word cards with definition cards.

**5.** *Observation.* Observe your students' use of new words in their speaking and writing. Ask them about words in their individual or class dictionaries.

**6.** *Teacher tests.* Sometimes you may want to construct a short test of "words of the week," for example, using any of the formats described in this chapter. A cautionary note: remember that your elementary and middle school students are not lexicographers. Asking them to write dictionary-type definitions is very difficult, and students often cannot do it even for words whose meanings they know quite well.

**7.** *Ask students.* Perhaps one of the best ways to determine if students know a word is to ask them whether or not they do. You can do this with individuals or with groups. You might simply say, "Here is a list of words. Tell me which ones you would like help with. Circle the words you don't know at all, and check the words you know for sure." Chances are, the information you get from this self-report will be just as accurate and reliable as what you would get from a test.

In Chapter 8, the focus shifts from vocabulary and its acquisition, use, and pedagogy to a look at the English language's abundant vocabulary. The chapter explores just a handful of our two million words, but they are words used flawlessly, magnificently, brilliantly, and they are words just waiting for you to use them. You are invited to sit back and enjoy the words to come.

## References

Aitchison, J. (1994). *Words in the mind: An introduction to the mental lexicon* (2nd ed.). Oxford, UK: Blackwell.

Buros, O. (1978). *The eighth mental measurement yearbook.* Highland Park, NJ: The Gryphon Press.

Miller, G. (1996). *The science of words.* New York: Scientific American Library.

# The Vitality of Words

## Samplings for Logophiles

*Words are, of course, the most powerful drug used by mankind.*

—Rudyard Kipling

It is fitting to approach the conclusion of a book about vocabulary by letting words speak for themselves. In this penultimate chapter, you are invited to savor the strengths and joys and the precision and versatility of words, for through words, the wit and wisdom of humankind is shared and understood. In these pages you will find quotations worth remembering, words we have lived by, words of wisdom, lists of words that reveal the spices of our lives, and words about words. There will be no overt pedagogy in this chapter, no reference to theory, research, or practical application. But you will learn something, I predict, and maybe a good deal, if you take the time to wander through it and enjoy the delights of words and words used well. You might want to make charts with some of the examples, titled by category headings, to be displayed around the room for student reference. The reference works that I found to be most helpful are listed at the end of this chapter.

## Words to Be Remembered

Simply put, some spoken words are memorable. The sampling of quotations in this section have given the world wisdom or wit or both:

"That old law about 'an eye for an eye' leaves everybody blind."—Martin Luther King Jr.

"No one can make you feel inferior without your consent."—Eleanor Roosevelt

"People will believe anything if you whisper it."—Anonymous

"Everyone is ignorant, only on different subjects."—Will Rogers

"Experience is a hard teacher. She gives the test first."—Anonymous

"The time to win a fight is before it starts."—Frederick W. Lewis

"The real purpose of books is to trick the mind into doing its own thinking."—Christopher Morley

"Don't wait for George to do it because he won't."—Jessica Julian

"It has ever been my experience that folks who have no vices have very few virtues."—Abraham Lincoln

"If you are not part of the solution, you are part of the problem."—Eldridge Cleaver

"To teach is to learn twice."—Joseph Joubert

"Freedom is not worth having if it does not include the freedom to make mistakes."—Mahatma Gandhi

"Common sense is genius dressed in its working clothes."—Ralph Waldo Emerson

"Nothing in life is to be feared. It is only to be understood."—Marie Curie

"The classroom—not the trench—is the frontier of freedom now and forevermore."—Lyndon Baines Johnson

"Pleasure is very seldom found where it is sought."—Samuel Johnson

"First health, then wealth, then pleasure, and do not owe anything to anybody."—Catherine the Great

"Truth is such a rare thing, it is delightful to tell it."—Emily Dickinson

"Life appears to me to be too short to be spent in nursing animosity or registering wrongs."—Charlotte Brontë

"The only certainty is that nothing is certain."—Pliny the Elder

"Instead of loving your enemies, treat your friends a little better."—Edgar Watson Home

"The only thing more expensive than education is ignorance."—Benjamin Franklin

"Don't compromise yourself. You're all you've got."—Janis Joplin

"My knowledge is like a drop in a vast ocean of promise."—Tan Sen

"People change and forget to tell each other."—Lillian Hellman

"Today is the first day of the rest of your life."—Abbie Hoffman

"Advice is what we ask for when we already know the answer but wish we didn't."—Erica Jong

"Success comes before work only in the dictionary."—Anonymous

"It ain't over till it's over."—Yogi Berra

"He who laughs, lasts."—Mary Pettibone Poole

"Income tax returns are the most imaginative fiction being written today."—Herman Wouk

"Never eat more than you can lift."—Miss Piggy

"A good deed never goes unpunished."—Gore Vidal

"I don't care what is written about me so long as it isn't true."—Dorothy Parker

"I wish Frank Sinatra would just shut up and sing."—Lauren Bacall

"Success didn't spoil me; I've always been insufferable."—Fran Lebowitz

"History will be kind to me for I intend to write it."—Winston Churchill

"Some editors are failed writers, but so are most writers."—T. S. Eliot

"If you want a place in the sun, prepare to put up with a few blisters."—Abigail van Buren

"If the phone doesn't ring, it's me."—Jimmy Buffett

"The trouble with the rat race is that even if you win you're still a rat."—Lily Tomlin

"Somebody left the cork out of my lunch."—W. C. Fields

"University politics are vicious precisely because the stakes are so small."—Henry Kissinger

"It's so beautifully arranged on the plate—you know someone's fingers have been all over it."—Julia Child

"If you can see the light at the end of the tunnel you are looking the wrong way."—Barry Commoner

"I hate small towns because once you've seen the cannon in the park there is nothing else to do."—Lenny Bruce

"Writers should be read, but neither seen nor heard."—Daphne Du Maurier

"I don't know anything about music. In my line you don't have to."—Elvis Presley

"Cats are intended to teach us that not everything in nature has a function."—Garrison Keillor

"Never go to a doctor whose office plants have died."—Erma Bombeck

"A statesman is a politician who has been dead ten or fifteen years."—Harry S Truman

"Even if you're on the right track, you'll get run over if you just sit there."—Will Rogers

## Words We Live By

Much of everyday life is guided by the mottoes, inscriptions, slogans, and laws that are part of our culture. The following examples are but a few of the thousands that have shaped our history.

### Mottoes

"North to the Future" (Alaska)

"Liberty and Independence" (Delaware)

"Union, Justice, and Confidence" (Louisiana)

"Live Free or Die" (New Hampshire)

"Friendship" (Texas)

"Forward" (Wisconsin)

"Independence, Pride, Dignity" (American Association of Retired Persons)

"We Shall Overcome" (American Civil Rights Movement)

"To serve, to strive, and not to yield" (Outward Bound)

"Faster, Higher, Stronger" (Olympic Games)

"Be prepared." (Boy Scouts)

"Do a good turn daily." (Girl Scouts)

### Inscriptions

"MAY THIS STRUCTURE, THRONED ON IMPERISHABLE BOOKS, BE MAINTAINED AND CHERISHED FROM GENERATION TO GENERATION FOR THE IMPROVEMENT AND DELIGHT OF MANKIND"—San Francisco Public Library

"THE PLACE OF JUSTICE IS A HALLOWED PLACE"—Department of Justice Building, Washington, D.C.

"THIS IS A GOVERNMENT OF LAW NOT OF MEN"—Orleans Parish Criminal Court House, New Orleans

"HERE RESTS IN HONORED GLORY AN AMERICAN SOLDIER KNOWN BUT TO GOD"—Tomb of the Unknown Soldier, Arlington National Cemetery

## Slogans

"Join or Die" (support for the thirteen colonies, 1754)

"Don't Tread on Me" (Colonial Virginia, 1755)

"Buy American" (following War of 1812, 1816)

"Tippecanoe and Tyler Too" (campaign for Harrison and Tyler, 1840)

"Henry Clay Will Carry the Day" (campaign for Henry Clay, 1844)

"Pikes Peak or Bust" (Colorado Gold Rush, 1859)

"Ballots for Both" and "I Wish Ma Could Vote" (women's suffrage movement, 1880s)

"Remember the Maine" (used to incite anger toward Spain, 1898)

"He Kept Us Out of War" (campaign for Woodrow Wilson, 1916)

"The War to End War" (World War I, 1917)

"A Chicken in Every Pot" (campaign for Herbert Hoover, 1928)

"In Hoover We Trusted, Now We Are Busted" (campaign for Franklin D. Roosevelt, 1932)

"Remember Pearl Harbor" (used to incite anger toward Japan, 1941)

"Loose Lips Sink Ships" (World War II, 1942)

"Phooey on Dewey" (campaign for Harry S Truman, 1948)

"I Like Ike" (campaign for Dwight D. Eisenhower, 1952)

"In Your Heart You Know He's Right" (campaign for Barry Goldwater, 1964)

"In Your Guts You Know He's Nuts" (campaign for Lyndon Johnson, 1964)

"Happy Birthday, America" (America's Bicentennial, 1976)

"Just Say No" (used by First Lady Nancy Reagan to combat youth drug use, 1988)

## Laws

"Work expands to fill the time available for its completion."—C. Northcote Parkinson

"The time spent on any item of an agenda will be in inverse proportion to its importance."—C. Northcote Parkinson

"In a hierarchy every employee tends to rise to his level of incompetence."—Laurence J. Peter

"In time, every post tends to be occupied by an employee who is incompetent to carry out its duties."—Laurence J. Peter

"If anything can go wrong it will."—Captain E. Murphy

## Words of Wisdom: American Proverbs

Proverbs are thought to contain the wisdom of the ancients, and there is no language, culture, or ethnic group that does not use proverbs to give advice or make observations. But not all proverbs are ancient. These proverbs are believed to be American in origin:

Money doesn't grow on trees.
A bad penny always turns up.
If the shoe fits, wear it.
Oil and water don't mix.
An apple never falls far from the tree.
Cream always rises to the top.
It is easy to repeat but hard to originate.
Talk is cheap.
We never feel the shoe unless it pinches our own foot.
Don't cross the bridge until you come to it.
The show must go on.
Nothing succeeds like success.
Better to be a big fish in a small pond than a little fish in a big pond.
Build a better mousetrap and the world will beat a path to your door.
Much profit, much risk.
Fish or cut bait.
Let the chips fall where they may.
All words are pegs to hang ideas on.
It's always fair weather when good friends get together.
There's always room at the top.
Curiosity killed the cat.
A good offense is the best defense.
You can't unscramble eggs.
Don't judge a book by its cover.
Don't take any wooden nickels.
Money can't buy happiness.
Don't stick your neck out.
One who slings mud loses ground.
The best things in life are free.
A picture is worth a thousand words.
If you can't beat 'em, join 'em.
You are what you eat.
The reward is in the doing.
The truth hurts.
Another day, another dollar.
Behind the clouds the sun is shining.
To know everything is to know nothing.

Friends you can count on you can count on your fingers.
Don't waste ten dollars looking for a dime.
The same sun that will melt butter will harden clay.
Never tell tales out of school.
It's not whether you win or lose but how you play the game.
Don't count your chickens before they're hatched.
If you lie down with dogs you'll get up with fleas.
There is no such thing as a free lunch.
Money talks.

## Words of Wisdom from around the World

The following proverbs originated in various lands and languages. Even in English translation, you will find sagacity in their simplicity.

When the cart breaks down, advice is plentiful. (Armenian)

The thief is sorry he is to be hanged, not that he is a thief. (English)

If you cannot catch a fish, do not blame the sea. (Greek)

The heaviest ear of corn is the one with its head bent low. (Irish)

Lovely flowers fade fast, weeds last the season. (Swedish)

From a short pleasure comes a long repentance. (French)

Make thyself a sheep and the wolf is ready. (Russian)

Of what you see, believe very little. Of what you are told, believe nothing. (Spanish)

He who was bitten by a snake avoids tall grass. (Chinese)

The dry reed does not seek the company of the fire. (Arabian)

Trust in God, but tie your camel. (Persian)

Better to lose your eye than your good name. (Armenian)

They who hold the ladder are as bad as the thief. (German)

Do not spit into the well—you may have to drink out of it. (Russian)

There are forty kinds of lunacy, but only one kind of common sense. (West African)

Eagles fly alone but sheep flock together. (Scottish)

If it is difficult to know a person, find out with whom he associates. You will then know him. (Yugoslavian)

He that blows in the fire must expect sparks in the eyes. (German)

A good reputation sits still, a bad one runs about. (Russian)

A trout in the pot is worth two salmon in the sea. (Irish)

A cow must graze where it is tied. (West African)

They who fall into the sea will cling even to a snake. (Turkish)

If every day were a sunny day, who would not wish for rain? (Japanese)

They that killeth when drunk are hanged when they are sober. (English)

If envy would burn, there would be no use of wood. (Yugoslavian)

The peasant reaches heaven as soon as the noble. (German)

To know the road ahead, ask those coming back. (Chinese)

No chicken will fall into the fire a second time. (West African)

Do not order the tree to be cut down which gives you shade. (Persian)

Friendship is a plant we must often water. (German)

One cannot learn to swim in a field. (Spanish)

Evil enters like a needle and spreads like an oak tree. (West African)

Water and words are easy to pour but impossible to recover. (Chinese)

A person is a guest for one or two days but becomes an intruder on the third. (Hindu)

When the ship has sunk, everyone knows how she could have been saved. (Italian)

Happiness rarely keeps company with an empty stomach. (Japanese)

You can't make a silk purse out of a sow's ear. (English)

A sleeping cat cannot catch a rat. (Indian)

He who would sweep the hut must not sit on the broom. (West African)

Laws, like a spider's web, catch the fly and let the hawk go free. (Russian)

The heaviest rains fall on the leakiest house. (Japanese)

## *Words from the Four Corners of the Earth*

English is such an adaptable language, it absorbs words from every continent and makes them its own. These words are but a tiny sample of the scores of words that have come from other languages to add to the richness of English.

| | |
|---|---|
| à la carte (French) | oregano (Spanish) |
| apartheid (Afrikaans) | orzo (Italian) |
| bildungsroman (German) | panzer (German) |
| bimbo (Italian) | paprika (Hungarian) |

chili (Spanish)
czar (Russian)
data (Latin)
diva (Italian)
embarrass (French)
ethos (Greek)
hari-kari (Japanese)
hyperbole (Latin)
igloo (Inuit)
iota (Greek)
jai alai (Basque)
judo (Japanese)
kayak (Inuit)
kibbutz (Hebrew)
lasagna (Italian)
leprechaun (Irish)
mambo (Yoruba)
minaret (Arabic)

quantum (Latin)
quiche (French)
ramen (Chinese)
ricotta (Italian)
sauna (Finnish)
sherbet (Turkish)
taboo (Tongan)
tepee (Sioux)
ukelele (Hawaiian)
ultimatum (Latin)
vaudeville (French)
virtuoso (Italian)
wampum (Algonquin)
wok (Chinese)
yenta (Yiddish)
yoga (Sanskrit)
Zeitgeist (German)
zombie (Bantu)

## Words from the Arts

Words enable us to describe and communicate about the aesthetic qualities that give us pleasure. The following short list of words identifies some categories of the fine arts.

### Architecture

| | | |
|---|---|---|
| Tudor | Baroque | Colonial |
| Federal | Georgian | Churrigueresque |
| Palladin | Rococo | Gothic |
| Art Deco | Art Nouveau | Bauhaus |
| Antebellum | | |

### Music

| | | |
|---|---|---|
| Chant | Folk | Chamber |
| Concerto | Étude | March |
| Opera | Sonata | Symphony |
| Bossa Nova | Cajun | Gospel |
| Dixieland | Reggae | Zydeco |
| Bluegrass | Hip Hop | Scat |
| Ragtime | | |

### Dance

| | | |
|---|---|---|
| Ballet | Ballroom | Modern |
| Clog | Tango | Limbo |
| Waltz | Rumba | |

*Painting and Sculpture*

| | | |
|---|---|---|
| Realism | Symbolism | Impressionism |
| Pointillism | Fauvism | Expressionism |
| Cubism | Dadaism | Bauhaus |
| Surrealism | Kinetic | Abstract |
| Pop Art | Paleolithic | Mesopotamian |
| Classical | Byzantine | Carolingian |
| Romanesque | Islamic | Gothic |
| Renaissance | Baroque | Rococo |

*Literature*

| | | |
|---|---|---|
| Fable | Fiction | Novella |
| Roman à clef | Romance | Saga |
| Biography | Doctrine | Oration |
| Polemic | Poetry | Ballad |
| Ode | Allegorical | Children's |
| Farce | Parody | Lampoon |
| Melodrama | Tragedy | Tragicomedy |
| Ballad | | |

## Words for Worry: Phobias

It seems that we can always find something to worry about. Phobias are persistent, strong, and sometimes illogical fears or dislikes of specific things. The following words delineate some of our many phobias.

*Travel*

bridges—gephyrophobia     crossing streets—dromophobia
flying—aerophobia     speed—tachophobia
train travel—amaxophobia     walking—basiphobia

*Situations*

being alone—monophobia     crowds—demophobia
enclosed spaces—claustrophobia     going to bed—clinophobia
heights—acrophobia     home—domatophobia
open spaces—agoraphobia     school—scholionophobia
shadows—sciophobia     standing—stasophobia

*Food and Drink*

alcohol—potophobia     drinking—dipsophobia
eating—phagophobia     food—sitophobia
meat—carnophobia

### Animals and Plants

bees—apiphobia
dogs—cynophobia
flowers—anthophobia
insects—entomophobia
parasites—parisitophobia
spiders—arachnophobia
wasps—spheksophobia

birds—ornithophobia
fish—ichthyophobia
fur—doraphobia
mice—musophobia
snakes—ophidophobia
trees—dendrophobia
worms—helminthophobia

### The Elements

flood—antlophobia
ice—cryophobia
rain—ombrophobia
thunder—brontophobia

fog—homichlophobia
lightning—astraphobia
snow—chionophobia
wind—ancraophobia

### Inanimate Objects

books—bibliophobia
machinery—mechanophobia
mirrors—eisoptrophobia
needles—belonophobia
string—linonophobia

glass—nelophobia
metals—metallophobia
money—chrometophobia
pins—enetephobia

### The Senses

being dirty—automysophobia
blushing—ereuthophobia
fatigue—kopophobia
itching—acarophobia
odors—osmophobia
pleasure—hedonophobia
smothering—pnigerophobia
stings—cnidophobia
trembling—tremophobia

being touched—haphephobia
cold—cheimatophobia
heat—thermophobia
noise—phonophobia
pain—algophobia
sleep—hypnophobia
speaking—lalophobia
taste—geumatophobia

### Health and Anatomy

beards—pogonophobia
childbirth—tocophobia
germs—spermophobia
knees—genuphobia
skin—dermatophobia
vomiting—emetophobia

blood—haematophobia
death—necrophobia
insanity—lyssophobia
poison—toxiphobia
teeth—odontophobia
wounds—traumatophobia

### Others

darkness—nyctophobia

daylight—phengophobia

dirt—mysophobia
everything—pantophobia
ghosts—phasmophobia
words—logophobia

disorder—ataxiophobia
fire—pyrophobia
rust—iophobia
writing—graphophobia

## Words for Ways to Play

Life isn't all worry—or work. It is good for the body, mind, and spirit to take time for play. This is a list of words for some kinds of play enjoyed by many of us.

| | | |
|---|---|---|
| baseball | flying | downhill skiing |
| football | judo | pentathlon |
| rugby | rowing | cross-country skiing |
| soccer | figure skating | softball |
| cricket | speed skating | swimming |
| ice hockey | roller skating | marathon running |
| field hockey | roller blading | biathlon |
| basketball | snowshoeing | bobsledding |
| volleyball | curling | tennis |
| tobogganing | luge | hardball |
| riding horses | fishing | squash |
| racing horses | pool | billiards |
| snooker | racketball | harness racing |
| golf | lacrosse | pole vaulting |
| bowling | shuffleboard | table tennis |
| broad jumping | mountaineering | badminton |
| long jumping | spelunking | discus throw |
| snowboarding | water polo | hammer throw |
| skateboarding | javelin throw | camping |
| diving | shot put | checkers |
| skindiving | hang gliding | wrestling |
| weightlifting | board games | parachuting |
| water skiing | gymnastics | word games |

## Words for the Appetite

Most of us enjoy good food. English abounds in words that differentiate the countless varieties of food that can be found. Perhaps you are planning a picnic. Words will help you specify which pasta and herbs to include in the casserole, which breads and cheeses for the basket, and, of course, the appropriate desserts.

### Pasta

| | | |
|---|---|---|
| macaroni | cannelloni | pennini |
| baby shells | penne | cappelletti |
| elbows | seeds | tortellini |
| ravioli | turrets | noodles |
| lasagna | mafalde | mozzani |
| linguini | manicotti | lumache |
| alphabet | wheels | ditali |
| stars | bows | big shells |
| gemelli | rings | agnolotti |
| ziti | angel hair | vermicelli |
| fedelini | orzo | corkscrew |

### Herbs

| | | |
|---|---|---|
| basil | tarragon | chervil |
| parsley | marjoram | sweet bay |
| oregano | sage | rosemary |
| savory | thyme | dill |
| mint | louvage | hyssop |
| borage | nasturtium | lemon balm |

### Breads

| | | |
|---|---|---|
| Vienna | Irish soda | corn |
| French | milk | whole wheat |
| challah | croissant | Scandinavian crak |
| Indian chapati | American white | caraway seed |
| pumpernickel | Danish rye | German rye |
| black rye | Indian naan | pita |
| multigrain | cheese | cinnamon |
| bagel | biscuit | Dakota roll |

### Cheeses

| | | |
|---|---|---|
| Cheddar | Monterey jack | brick |
| liederkranz | Roquefort | boursault |
| brie | colby | jalapeno |
| Camembert | Muenster | Swiss |
| Jarlsberg | havarti | Gruyere |
| comte | pepper | Limburger |

### Desserts

| | | |
|---|---|---|
| cakes | pies | tarts |
| bars | ice cream | donuts |
| cream puffs | sherbets | petits fours |
| eclairs | mousse | brioche |

| jelly rolls | custards | parfaits |
| cookies | puddings | candies |

## Words for Worship

Worship plays an important part in some people's lives. As with everything else, words help us differentiate our beliefs and explain them to others.

### Major Religions and Denominations

| | | |
|---|---|---|
| Bahaism | Buddhism | Theravada |
| Judaism | Tibetan | Christian |
| Anglican | Baptist | Church of Christ |
| Congregational | Luthern | Methodist |
| Russian Orthodox | Ethiopian Orthodox | Greek Orthodox |
| Romanian Orthodox | Pentecostal | Presbyterian |
| Roman Catholic | Unitarian | United Churches |
| Christian Scientists | Mennonite | Confucianism |
| Hindu | Vishnu | Shiva |
| Shakti | Islam | Sunni |
| Shiism | Sufi | Ismaili |
| Jainism | Digambara | Swetabara |
| Jehovah's Witnesses | Mahayana | Mormon |
| Scientology | Seventh Day Adventists | Shintoism |
| Sikhism | Society of Friends | Spiritualism |
| Taoism | Unification | Zorastrianism |
| Hari Krishna | Chinese Folk | Animism |

### Seven Deadly Sins

| | |
|---|---|
| Pride | Covetousness |
| Anger | Gluttony |
| Sloth | Lust |
| Envy | |

### Five Cardinal Virtues

| | |
|---|---|
| Jen, Benevolence | Yi, Duty |
| Chih, Wisdom | Hism, Faithfulness |
| Li, Manners | |

### Four Aims of Life

| | |
|---|---|
| Dharma, Right Conduct | Artha, Material Gain |
| Kama, Pleasure | Moksa, Liberation |

## Words We Seldom Use

There are numerous perfectly useful words that are rarely used or have become obsolete even though they convey explicit meanings. How many of the following words do you know? Do you use them? If you know and use more than 15 of them, you truly are a logophile. Some certainly will send you to an uncommonly big dictionary.

| | | |
|---|---|---|
| tarantism | tuatara | gleet |
| nostomania | codgel | scurfy |
| acronyx | vermiform | philoneist |
| gronk | misandronist | misopolemiac |
| saccade | Luddite | chafferer |
| zoonosis | higgler | jowter |
| olecranon | arctophilist | oologist |
| bibulous | timbromaniac | ascian |
| accubation | blatherskite | blatteroon |
| cleptobiosis | marshaller | nacket |
| groak | swoophead | polymath |
| parorexia | troglodyte | wowser |
| meacock | allotheism | theriolatry |
| gump | zucchetto | psephology |
| tatterdemalion | malversation | snurge |
| mome | clusterfist | swedge |
| Pecksniff | intrapreneur | pismirism |
| cosherer | trantles | logophile |
| snuffler | logomaniac | aeolist |
| cullion | phrontistery | quodlibetarian |
| lickspittle | sophist | anoegenetic |
| snarge | algology | eremology |
| lolaby | nostology | piscatology |
| bandicoot | proxemics | chirr |
| wanderoo | jargle | rataplan |
| blatoid | obmutescent | ipsedixitism |
| porcine | parapraxis | anthropoglot |

## Words and Our Animal Friends

Many English words describe or are adapted from the animal kingdom. We have distinct collective nouns for groups of animals; different, often onomatopoeic, words for their voices; and separate words for their offspring.

Some of our well-known idioms, similes, slang, and slogans contain animal references.

### Groups of Animals

| | | |
|---|---|---|
| herd of antelope | army of ants | cete of badgers |
| swarm of bees | brace of bucks | clowder of cats |
| brood of chickens | bed of clams | murder of crows |
| litter of cubs | pack of dogs | paddling of ducks |
| herd of elephants | gang of elks | school of fish |
| skulk of foxes | gaggle of geese | skein of geese |
| band of gorillas | cast of hawks | drift of hogs |
| husk of rabbits | smack of jellyfish | troop of kangaroos |
| exaltation of larks | pride of lions | plague of locusts |
| labor of moles | watch of nightingales | yoke of oxen |
| covey of partridges | muster of peacocks | nide of pigeons |
| litter of pigs | string of ponies | pod of porpoises |
| pack of rats | flock of sheep | host of sparrows |
| mustering of storks | knot of toads | hover of trout |
| rafter of turkeys | bale of turtles | pack of wolves |
| descent of woodpeckers | | |

### Animal Offspring

| | | |
|---|---|---|
| antelope—calf | bear—cub | beaver—kit |
| bird—fledgling | cat—kitten | deer—fawn |
| duck—duckling | eagle—eaglet | fowl—chick |
| fox—cub | frog—polliwog | goat—kid |
| goose—gosling | hen—pullet | horse—foal |
| kangaroo—joey | lion—cub | mackerel—blinker |
| owl—owlet | partridge—cheeper | pig—shoat |
| pigeon—squab | rabbit—bunny | rat—pup |
| salmon—parr | swan—cygnet | tiger—whelp |
| turkey—poult | whale—calf | zebra—foal |

### Animal Sounds

| | | |
|---|---|---|
| apes—gibber | bears—growl | bees—buzz |
| beetles—drone | birds—sing | bulls—bellow |
| calves—bleat | cats—meow | chicks—peep |
| cows—moo | crows—caw | dogs—bark |
| dolphins—click | doves—coo | ducks—quack |
| eagles—scream | elephants—trumpet | flies—buzz |
| foxes—bark | frogs—croak | geese—cackle |
| grasshoppers—chirp | grouse—drum | guinea fowl—cry |
| guinea pigs—squeak | gulls—squawk | hares—squeak |
| horses—whinny | hyenas—laugh | jays—chatter |

lions—roar
monkeys—gibber
oxen—low
pigeons—coo
rhinoceroses—snort
snakes—hiss
swans—cry
turkeys—gobble

loons—howl
nightingales—pipe
parrots—talk
pigs—grunt
roosters—crow
stags—bellow
tigers—roar
wolves—howl

mice—squeak
owls—hoot
peacocks—scream
ravens—croak
sheep—bleat
swallows—titter
turtles—grunt

## Animal Verbs

to ape
to bull
to ferret
to hawk
to lionize
to rook

to badger
to clam up
to flounder
to hog
to monkey with
to snipe

to buffalo
to duck
to gander
to horse around
to rat
to squirrel away

## Animal Sayings

bats in your belfry
to bell the cat
a bird in the hand . . .
busy as a bee
cat has nine lives
Charley horse
cook your goose
cry wolf
dead as a dodo
to eat crow
fine kettle of fish
fish out of water
get one's goat
go hog wild
go to the dogs
goose pimples
hang-dog look
happy as a lark
hold your horses
hot dog
to hound someone
in the doghouse
kangaroo court
living high off the hog
to play possum
red herring

a bee in one's bonnet
bull in a china shop
to pass the buck
cast pearls before swine
chicken in every pot
chicken feed
sow down
eager beaver
drink like a fish
every dog has its day
fly in the ointment
beat a dead horse
get on one's high horse
a gone goose
go whole hog
hair of the dog
hog wash
have a lark
horse of a different color
I smell a rat
hush puppy
dog days of summer
pig out
mad as a wet hen
putting on the dog
toady

| | |
|---|---|
| sacred cow | stool pigeon |
| turkey | don't look a gift horse in the mouth |
| don't change horses . . . | |

## Words about Words

I close this chapter with quotations from philosophers, authors, teachers, and others who have made potent use of words to express their feelings about words.

"No iron can pierce the heart with the force of a well-placed phrase."—Isaac Babel

"But words are things, and a small drop of ink,
Falling like dew, upon a thought, produces
That which, makes thousands, perhaps millions,
think."—Lord Byron

"The whole world opened to me when I learned to read."—Mary McLeod Bethune

"Of all the human relaxations which are free from guilt, none is so dignified as reading."—Edgerton Brydges

"A room without books is a body without a soul."—Marcus Tullius Cicero

"It is not pathetic passages that make us shed our best tears, but the miracle of a word in the right place."—Jean Cocteau

"Readers are leaders. Thinkers succeed."—Marva Collins

"A blemish may be taken out of the diamond by careful polishing; but if your words have the least blemish, there is no way to efface it."—Confucius

"The best of my education has come from the public library . . . my tuition fee is a bus fare and once in a while, five cents a day for an overdue book. You don't need to know very much to start with, if you know the way to the public library."—Lesley Conger

"A library is the delivery room for the birth of ideas, a place where history comes to life."—Norman Cousins

"One must be drenched in words, literally soaked in them, to have the right ones form themselves into the proper pattern at the right moment."—Hart Crane

"Whatever the costs of our libraries, the price is cheap compared to that of an ignorant nation."—Walter Cronkite

"Books are the quietest and most constant of friends; they are the most accessible and wisest of counselors, and the most patient of teachers."—Charles W. Eliot

"When I read a good book . . . I wish that life were three thousand years long."—Ralph Waldo Emerson

"A university is just a group of buildings gathered around a library."—Shelby Foote

"If I couldn't read, I couldn't live."—Thelma Green

"The great gift is the passion for reading. It is cheap, it consoles, it distracts, it excites, it gives you knowledge of the world and experience of a kind."—Elizabeth Hardwick

"What in the world would we do without our libraries?"—Katharine Hepburn

"The time to read is anytime: no apparatus, no appointment of time and place, is necessary. It is the only art which can be practiced at any hour of the day or night, whenever the time and inclination comes, that is your time for reading; in joy or sorrow, health or illness."—Holbrook Jackson

"No entertainment is so cheap as reading, nor any pleasure so lasting."—Lady Mary Wortley Montagu

"I know not how to abstain from reading."—Samuel Pepys

"A great book should leave you with many experiences and slightly exhausted at the end. You live several lives while reading it."—William Styron

"Books are the carriers of civilization. Without books, history is silent, literature dumb, science crippled, thought and speculation at a standstill."—Barbara W. Tuchman

"When I was about eight, I decided that the most wonderful thing, next to a human being, was a book."—Margaret Walker

"I conceive that a knowledge of books is the basis on which all other knowledge rests."—George Washington

"Humanity and patriotism both cry aloud for books, books, books."—Mason Locke Weems

"My alma mater was books, a good library . . . I could spend the rest of my life reading, just satisfying my curiosity."—Malcolm X

It was my intent that the present chapter display the magnificence of words. Can you contemplate a society without a language? What would a world be like in which there were no words with which to communicate?

The words of Eve Clark that began this book seem a fitting way to end it: "Words are the starting point . . ."

This book concludes with a chapter about word and language play that stresses the importance of helping children enjoy the wonderful world of words.

## *References*

Bettman, O. L. (1987). *The delights of reading: Quotes, notes & anecdotes.* Boston: David R. Godine, Publisher.

Burrell, B. (1997). *The words we live by: The creeds, mottoes, and pledges that have shaped America.* New York: The Free Press.

Byrne, R. (1988). *1,911 best things anybody ever said.* New York: Fawcett Columbine.

Corbeil, J. C. (1986). *The Facts on File visual dictionary.* New York: Facts on File Publications.

Elster, C. H. (1996). *There's a word for it! A grandiloquent guide to life.* New York: Scribner.

Fergusson, R. (1983). *The Penguin dictionary of proverbs.* London, UK: Penguin Books.

Gleason, N. (1992). *Proverbs from around the world.* New York: Citadel Press.

Graffagnino, J. K. (1996). *Only in books: Writers, readers, & bibliophiles on their passion.* Madison, WI: Madison House Publishers.

Hendrickson, R. (1983). *Animal crackers: A bestial lexicon.* New York: The Viking Press.

Johnson, B. V. (in press). *Word works: Exploring language play.* Golden, CO: Fulcrum Press.

Kipfer, B. A. (1997, 1998). *The order of things: How everything in the world is organized into hierarchies, structures, and pecking orders.* New York: Random House.

Mieder, W., Kingsbury, S. A., & Harder, K. B. (Eds.). (1992). *A dictionary of American proverbs.* New York: Oxford University Press.

Titelman, G. Y. (1996). *Random House dictionary of popular proverbs and sayings.* New York: Random House.

# 9

## *Our Fascination with Words*

### *Word Play in the Classroom*

Can you solve these three different kinds of word-play riddles? Their answers can be found on page 144.

**A.** Identify the missing words by using the number and the first letters to complete the expression.

**Example:** 18 = h.__ on a g.__ c.__ (holes on a golf course)

1. 26 = l.__ of the a.__
2. 13 = s.__ on the A.__ f.__
3. 1 = w.__ on a u.__
4. 5 or 9 = d.__ in a Z.__ C.__
5. 4 = p.__ on a c.__

**B.** Think of two one-syllable rhyming words to answer each question.

**Example:** What might cause bad bubbles? (bum gum)

6. What do you have when everyone cleans up?
7. What is the bird that brings baby pigs?
8. What might you call a terrified criminal?
9. Where might you keep valuable boards?
10. What do you do to make steaming hot mud?

**C.** Can you guess the occupations of the following individuals?

**Example:** Sally Ride (astronaut)

11. Roy Holler
12. Linda Toote
13. Elizabeth Shelver
14. O. O. Oops
15. Rollie Fingers

You may be wondering what such riddles have to do with vocabulary development or language learning. *The principal purpose of word and language play in the classroom or the home is to stimulate or sustain the natural interest in language that children exhibit practically from birth.* The ability to learn and use oral and written language and to add words to one's mental lexicon and retrieve them when needed is essential for efficient communication and intellectual achievement. These capacities are sharpened when undergirded by a sustained inquisitiveness about, exposure to, and use of the language.

Children enjoy exploring the sounds and rhythms of language (Humpty Dumpty sat on a wall). They laugh at "dumb" jokes (Why did the chicken), word repetitions (goody goody), and alliterative tongue twisters (Peter Piper picked a peck). Between their toddler years and their teens, youngsters experiment with their developing command of oral and written language. Somewhere, though, in the elementary and middle grades, learning language comes to be thought of as "work," not "play." Geller (1985) observed:

> For me, as an educator, the anomaly in this situation has been the absence of word play from the classroom—especially classrooms of the primary and middle elementary years. Teachers of these ages are aware of youngsters' penchant for play; however, most see no educational reason to bring it into the classroom. The question generally posed is, What does word play have to do with language education? or, more to the point: What does word play have to do with the teaching of reading and writing? (pp. 2–3)

People in all societies and cultures play word games, create nicknames, tell jokes, and write poems and jingles. Some find challenge in language riddles such as those that opened this chapter. Puns, codes, anagrams, and word creation are forms of word play of interest to others. The popularity of crossword puzzles and games such as *Scrabble, Mad Libs,* and *Pictionary* attests to the compelling lure of language.

This chapter is built on bedrock principles of learning: children learn best when they have strong personal interests in a topic, when they are motivated, and when they have teachers who hold high expectations for them (*What Works,* 1987, pp. 35, 37). Conversely, learners avoid, as much as possible, what does not interest them. I do not like to bowl or play croquet, so I never go near those sports. I love to read and garden, so I tend to do these things whenever I can find time. Children come to school with a language instinct and an innate preoccupation with using and manipulating language. A major challenge to teachers is to keep that interest high and strengthen it to the degree possible. This book is written to provide suggestions for vocabulary development in elementary and middle schools. Chapter 9 is written to describe word and language play activities that may help stimulate excitement about language and consequently enhance vocabulary development. Not all of the recommended teaching activities fit all age groups. Teachers know their students best and will determine which activities are worth trying. I chose to place the word play chapter at the end of the book to emphasize the importance of word play in any vocabulary development program.

In her introduction to *Playing with Words* (1987), child psychologist Margie Golick explained her reasons for including language play in her work with children:

> Language skill makes word play possible. Word games, in turn, further language development. They get children and adolescents talking and listening, thinking about the form and meaning of words and sentences. Furthermore, word games are fun, addictive, and a source of lifelong pleasure. Addict that I am, I use word play in my "work" with children. It has become the remedial tool I like best to get children and adolescents to develop their vocabulary, to improve their reading and spelling, and to sharpen their thinking skills. (p. 14)

Word play refers to any adaptation of words, their sounds, spellings, shapes, meanings, groupings, uses in expressions, or any other modifications that help achieve a humorous, descriptive, satirical, critical, or mentally challenging effect. This chapter describes seven broad categories of word play as shown in the following list.

### Seven Categories of Word Play

1. Onomastics (proper names)
2. Expressions (idioms, slang, etc.)
3. Figures of speech (personification, oxymorons, etc.)
4. Word associations (synonyms, antonyms, etc.)
5. Word formation (compounds, abbreviations, etc.)
6. Word shapes and spellings (anagrams, rebuses, etc.)
7. Word games (hink pinks, 20 questions, etc.)

Each of the seven categories is explained, subcategorized, and exemplified. One or two teaching activities are provided for the seven categories.

Before beginning our examination of onomastics, here are the answers to the riddles that opened the chapter.

1. letters of the alphabet
2. stripes on the American flag
3. wheel on a unicycle
4. digits in a Zip Code
5. points on a compass
6. less mess
7. a pork stork
8. a shook crook
9. in a plank bank
10. you boil soil
11. auctioneer
12. professional musician
13. librarian
14. surgeon
15. major league pitcher

## Onomastics

In his book *What's in a Name? Reflections of an Irrepressible Name Collector,* Dickson (1996) described the "John Q. Raspberry Memorial Collection of Names." The collection was developed by Leland Hilligoss, a reference librarian at the St. Louis Public Library, who had been asked by a client to help locate a Mr. John Q. Raspberry. Hilligoss became interested in colorful and unusual names, and over the years developed the Raspberry Collection with the help of other librarians. The Collection was loaned to Dickson who added unique names located by other name collectors. The following real names are representative of the several hundred presented by Dickson (pp. 81–87).

| | | |
|---|---|---|
| Ormand Bobo | Coy Ham | Ethel Oink |
| Blanch Branch | Tarzan Kush | Esther Oyster |
| Toni Chickaloni | Kasper Kwak | Peter J. J. Rabbit |
| Fremont Curd | Furbish Lousewort | Stella Stoops |
| Parvin Feaster | Perpetua McGurk | Scott Towle |
| Olga Flabbi | Thomas J. Numnum | King Tutt |

Everything has a name. A name is a nontechnical word for a person (boy, Chase), an animal (dog, Trixie), a place (state, Mississippi), or a thing (book, *Grapes of Wrath*). Common names designate general members of a class such as vegetables: carrots, onions, beans. Common names usually are listed and defined in good dictionaries. Proper names designate specific personal names (Barbara Jones), place names (Montpelier, Vermont), events (World Cup), institutions (Clark College), vehicles (Corrado), books (*The*

*Literacy Dictionary*), plays (*Cabaret*), paintings (*Mona Lisa*), musical compositions (*Stars and Stripes Forever*), businesses ("Franks and Steins"), and more. Unless famous or important (e.g., *Big Ben, the Liberty Bell, the Big Dipper, the White House*), most proper names will not be found in most dictionaries. There are eight subcategories of onomastics that lend themselves to wordplay classroom activities.

**First Names and Last Names.**   Children come to school knowing their own names and the names of family members, friends, some members of the community, television characters, and characters in books. Names of people intrigue them. Some first and last names are common, but others such as those in the Raspberry Collection are quite unique.

First names are those given to children at birth by parents or guardians. Last names (surnames) are inherited. A person's name often is a representation of cultural identity. Try to imagine a culture in which people had no names. Parents choose names for various reasons. Some first names are taken from the Bible (Rebecca, Ruth, Adam), from antiquity (Marcus, Julius), royalty (Elizabeth, Charles), Germanic languages (William, Emma), French (Louis, Monique), Celtic traditions (Barry, Brian, Sheila), literature and film (Bonnie, Scarlett, Harry, Clark), precious stones (Pearl, Ruby), flowers (Daisy, Rose), qualities (Joy, Hope, Faith), and many other sources. *A Dictionary of First Names* (Hanks & Hodges, 1995) presents historical and linguistic information about 7,000 first names from Aaltje to Zulekha.

By the same authors, *A Dictionary of Surnames* (1988) gives the origins and meanings of nearly 70,000 surnames. Some surnames originated by assigning the first name of the father (Johnson, Peterson), others came from topographic features (Hill, Beach), occupations (Hunter, Baker, Potter), seasons (May, Winter), status (Squire, King, Bishop), places (Jordan, Berlin), nationalities (Welsh, German), plants (Moss, Redfern), colors (Green, White), and other sources.

**Nicknames.**   A number of people have nicknames. Sometimes the nicknames are shortened forms of first names (Barb, Lor, Allie, Dan, Tim, Jim). Others come from physical features (Curly, Lefty, Slim), intelligence (Egghead, Dodo), sports prowess (Crazy Legs, Magic), personality traits (Stormin' Norman, Blabbermouth), intimacy (Babycakes), and affection (Tot, Angel). Dickson (1996) reported that nicknames were even in use in ancient Egypt, including the nicknames Red, Tiny, Frog, Lazy, and Big Head (p. 155).

World leaders have been given nicknames (Tricky Dick Nixon, Slick Willie Clinton, Useless Grant) as have other well-known persons (The King—Elvis Presley, Moses—Harriet Tubman). Some people give nicknames to their cars (the Beater, the Clunk), their pets (Tarzan, Fifi), and even their parents (Pops, S. E.).

*Pseudonyms.*   Writers, actors, and media persons sometimes use pseudonyms that are fictitious. Pseudonyms have been used to hide one's identity or gender, or because they were thought to be more pronounceable or memorable than one's given name. Mark Twain is the pseudonym, or "pen name," for Samuel Langhorne Clemens, Dr. Seuss for Theodore Seuss Geisel, and George Eliot for Mary Ann Evans. Bob Dylan's given name was Robert Zimmerman, and Fred Astaire's was Frederick Austerlitz.

*Eponyms.*   Eponyms are words that are named after people. For example, the Braille alphabet is named for Louis Braille, a blind teacher. Jules Leotard, a circus perfomer, wore snug tights that are now called leotards. The teddy bear was named for Teddy Roosevelt. There are several food eponyms named for their creators. Sylvester Graham gave us the graham cracker, and Caesar salad first was prepared by Caesar Cardini, a restaurant owner in Mexico. *Webster's New World Dictionary of Eponyms* (Douglas, 1990) describes the sources of hundreds of eponyms.

*Toponyms.*   In contrast to eponyms, toponyms are words named after places. Examples include *hamburger,* named for Hamburg, Germany; *bologna* from Bologna, Italy; and *duffel bags* from Duffel, Belgium.

*Aptronyms.*   Aptronyms are the given names of persons when those names seem particularly appropriate to the work the people do. Five aptronyms were among the riddles at the start of this chapter. The following are a few of the numerous aptronyms collected by Dickson (1996, pp. 26–33): Matt Batts, baseball player; Bernard D. Crook, police chief; John Razor, barber (nickname: "Safety"); Priscilla Flattery, publicist; Gary Player, golfer; Jay A. Posthumas, funeral director; Louise Rumpp, diet center manager.

*Place Names.*   Place names include the names of countries, states, towns and cities, streets, lakes and hills, and subdivisions. Certain place names are important to real estate dealers, contractors, status seekers, and buyers of property who worry about resale value. Place names raise some researchable questions. Would you rather own a place in Melody Lane Village or Hog Farm Acres? Are lanes, ways, boulevards, drives, terraces, and rows nicer sounding than streets, roads, and highways? Why is Second Street the most common street name in America—more common than First Street or Main Street (Ash, 1995, p. 207)? How many states have cities with "Pleasant" in the name? What are the origins of such town names as Luck, Wisconsin; Jackpot, Nevada; Rich, Mississippi; and Prosperity, West Virginia? How are Muck City, Alabama, and Quicksand, Kentucky, alike? Would you rather settle in Ordinary, Virginia; Odd, West Virginia; or Boring, Maryland? Why are there Berlins and Dublins in many states? Where did states and cities get their nicknames (the Badger State, the Bay State, the Big Apple, the Big Easy, the Windy City)?

*Names for Businesses.* Some businesses have very run-of-the-mill business names (Simpson's Furniture, Walker Pharmacy, Schuster & Sons, Wolf Clinic). Other businesses display some creativity and a sense of humor in their choice of a business name. Among the most clever business name creators are day-care centers (Small World, Grin-and-Grow, Kiddy College), restaurants (Weiner-Take-All, Wok In, Food-Man-Chew), hairdressers (Cut Loose, Tangles, Hair Port), music stores (All Ears, Hi Fi Fo Fum), and independent bookstores (Cover to Cover, Canterbury Tales).

Names can enhance the appeal of language for children and activate their vocabulary development.

## Teaching Suggestions

Onomastics, the study of proper names, is a field filled with possibilities for research projects by elementary and middle school students. The questions and ideas below are representative of those that can lend direction to student research in this form of word play.

**1.** *First and last names.* Compile lists of the first names and last names of students in the class, grade, or entire school. Count the number of students who have each name (e.g., Jason—7, La Tondra—4, Ashley—5, Smith—4, Beeson—1) to determine the most common first and last names in the group. How do the most common first names differ from those of twenty years ago? To find out, students can survey parents, relatives, or other adults who are at least twenty years older to find out the first names of children with whom they went to school. What can be learned from the list of common surnames? What can be surmised about ethnic backgrounds or emigration patterns? Exploring the White Pages of telephone directories can lead to surprising discoveries about last names. For example, I personally am acquainted with a T. Wheat, an S. Straw, and an M. Oats. I have worked with a K. Fish, an N. Marlin, and an R. Bass. What unusual surnames "pop out" of available phone books?

**2.** *Nicknames.* Students might want to compile lists of the nicknames of classmates, teachers, and others. The nicknames could be categorized according to physical features (tall Paul), personal traits (Whiz), affection (Punkin), shortened first name (Deb), or any other pattern that becomes apparent. Does your city or state have a nickname? How about local or favorite sports teams? Who or what else in the vicinity has a nickname?

**3.** *Eponyms.* Words named after people are called eponyms (e.g., *chicken tetrazzini* is named after Luisa Tetrazzini). Students with culinary skills might want to create recipes for favorite foods and name them for themselves or a family member (e.g., Eggs Clarinda, Junko Pudding, Rice Rollins).

**4.** *Aptronyms.* Aptronyms are the names of people that seem to match their occupations (e.g., Mary Lamb is the owner of Little Bo Peep children's bookstore). Can your students find any aptronyms in the business and professional listings in the Yellow Pages of the telephone book?

**5.** *Place names.* State highway maps and road atlases (including their indexes) are easy-to-come-by resources for research on place names. Questions to be answered might include: Which cities in your state are named for places in foreign countries? For presidents? For cities in other states? Which cities have Native American names? Hispanic names? French names? Which cities have unusual names? What do the answers to these questions suggest about the history of your state?

**6.** *Names for businesses.* Which businesses in your community have clever names? Once again, the Yellow Pages of the phone book may be the best resource. Completed lists will lead to a spirited discussion about why certain types of businesses tend to use creative names and why other types may not.

## Expressions

Five types of language expressions are in regular use in oral and written English: idioms, proverbs, slang, catchphrases, and slogans. These expressions have special meanings not predictable from the meanings of their individual words or word parts, or they are words that are used in unconventional ways. The five types are figurative expressions that help to make English more colorful and playful than does strictly literal expression.

*Idioms.*    The English language is enriched by its thousands of idiomatic expressions within the general lexicon. Idioms have meanings that are unique; they are not formed by combining the usual meanings of the words within the idiom. For this reason, idioms can pose major difficulties for students learning English as a second or foreign language. Consider the confusion that would come to someone who attributed literal meanings to the idioms in these sentences:

> The Stiles always seem *to rob Peter to pay Paul.*
> Try this casserole. It will *stick to your ribs.*
> How can he *hold his head up* after that display?
> Thomas seems to be *a little slow on the draw.*
> Finally, we began *to see the daylight.*

A collection of idioms that I have found particularly helpful in designing instruction is *NTC's Thematic Dictionary of American Idioms* (Spears, 1998). It presents meanings and context sentences for 353 pages of idioms organized in 900 themes. For example, under the theme "Adequacy-Lacking" are the idioms "not up to snuff," "wide of the mark," and "won't hold water" (p. 8). A recommended book for children ages 8 and up is the *Scholastic Dictionary of Idioms* (Terban, 1996). The *Dictionary* presents more than 600 idioms (e.g., "bite the bullet," "drop in the bucket," "egg on your face") together with definitions, origins of the idioms, sample sentences, and illustrations.

*Proverbs.* Proverbs are lasting, wise sayings that often are advisory in nature (e.g., *A bird in the hand is worth two in the bush*). Proverbs combine elements of idioms (expressions with unique meanings) and metaphors (expressions of comparison). Most languages and cultures use proverbs, and some different languages have proverbs of identical meaning. For example, English language speakers say, "Let sleeping dogs lie," and the French warn, "Don't bother a sleeping cat." Both mean that it is best to not stir up trouble.

Just as it is possible in life to get conflicting advice, some proverbs have contradictory meanings. One proverb says, "Too many cooks spoil the broth," but another one says, "Many hands make light work." Similarly "Easy come, easy go" is contradicted by "A penny saved is a penny earned," and "Out of sight, out of mind" by "Absence makes the heart grow fonder." Some proverbs have become so much a part of our cultural literacy that only a portion of the expression is sufficient to carry its meaning. "Yes, it would be a great promotion, but don't count your chickens . . ." (*Don't count your chickens before they hatch* means don't count on something before it actually occurs). A valuable resource for teachers is the *Dictionary of Proverbs and Their Origins* (Flavell & Flavell, 1993). The book presents etymologies of hundreds of common proverbs.

*Slang.* Slang often gets a bad rap in the schools, even though some teachers may talk about *Mickey Mouse* courses they have taken, and *airheads, windbags,* and administrative *pea brains* they have known. College students have long been credited for their slang contributions to the lexicon, and they continue to contribute. College slang of the 1990s included *squirrel kisser* (environmentalist), *McPaper* (a quickly written paper), and *word up* (I agree).

Slang should not be thought of as synonymous with vulgar language. Some slang is offensive, but most is not. Neither should slang be confused with technical jargon—the words used by practitioners of particular trades and professions (e.g., Educators speak of *multiple intelligences* and *induction*). Slang expressions usually have been created by the young, the socially alienated, by members of certain occupations, by the military branches and specialties, and by people who see themselves as members of unique groups.

Individuals enjoy using slang that only certain others understand because it suggests identity and exclusiveness.

Slang is used in every medium, and students cannot process oral or written language accurately unless they are familiar with slang expressions. I recommend two works to teachers seeking slang reference books. The first is the scholarly *Random House Historical Dictionary of American Slang* (Lighter, 1994, 1997, 2000). The first volume, *A–G*, contains more than 20,000 slang expressions. Lighter's work makes clear that slang has been in use a long time (e.g., "made in the shade"—1896, "homeboy"—1899, "longhair"—1920, "hippie"—1952, "out to lunch"—1955). An entertaining book that organizes slang expressions by user groups is *Idiom Savant: Slang as It Is Slung: The Colorful Lingo of American Subcultures, from Animators to Zine Readers* (Dunn, 1997). Some examples of slang used by airline flight attendants are "hockey pucks" (small steaks), "pilot pellets" (peanuts), "leather or feather" (steak or chicken), and "roach coach" (charter flight) (pp. 33–34).

*Catchphrases.*   Catchphrases are so named because their intent is to catch someone's attention. They probably "catch on" because they are more colorful expressions of ideas than ordinary literal language. Some catchphrases have short lifespans. (For example, "Very interesting . . . but stupid" was spoken weekly by Arte Johnson on the 1960s television show *Laugh In*. It became a popular expression of the times, but rarely has been heard in recent decades.) Other catchphrases catch on in small locations. Still other catchphrases have endured and become idioms. (For example, *No rest for the wicked* means to be inundated with work. It was popular in the 1900s and may have originated in the biblical book of Isaiah.) See the *Dictionary of Catchphrases* (Rees, 1995) for a listing of 1,200 catchphrases, together with their meanings and origins.

*Slogans.*   Slogans are catchphrases that have been created to help sell a product (e.g., "*Coke* is the real thing"), to promote an idea or cause (e.g., *Just Say No* was a slogan coined by former First Lady Nancy Reagan to urge young people not to use drugs), or for political purposes (e.g., *Phooey on Dewey* was used by supporters of Harry Truman when he ran against Thomas Dewey for U.S. President in 1948). Most slogans have come and gone with the products, ideas, or politics of the times.

All five expressions (i.e., idioms, proverbs, slang, catchphrases, and slogans) lend themselves to linguistic creativity and experimentation, ingredients used by elementary and middle schoolers who engage in word play.

## Teaching Suggestions

Idioms are plentiful in English; therefore, idiomatic word play serves a helpful function in language development, especially for students with limited

English proficiency. Each idiom represents a concept and must be learned as such. Your students rarely will encounter an idiom in isolation. Idioms take meaning from—and give meaning to—the sentences in which they occur. Provide students with a list of idioms embedded in age-appropriate sentences such as the following:

1. Ms. Herman said that when she wins the lottery, she'll be able to *ride the gravy train*.
2. Chantelle sent me on *a wild goose chase* because, after three hours of looking, I never did find the poster that she wanted.
3. When little Reginald didn't get to watch his favorite show, he *turned on the waterworks*.
4. I'd better start saving now because the concert will *cost a pretty penny*.
5. When Adriana was chosen to play the flute solo, it was *a feather in her cap*.
6. Marvin drove so slowly he *tied up traffic* for miles.
7. Carmen decided to *stick her neck out* and introduce herself to her new classmates.
8. Jean is such a moody person that you have *to walk on eggs* when she is around.
9. LeRoy told Raymond not to worry about their argument because it was *water under the bridge*.
10. After an hour of trudging through the snow, the cabin was *a sight for sore eyes*.

There is more to learning a word or an idiom than learning its definition. In fact, creating a definition is a specialized and difficult task. Context helps pin down the meaning of an idiom, so creating appropriate contexts may be the best way to play with its meaning.

Select a set of idioms in sentences such as those above. Ask pairs or small teams of students to discuss the idioms and generate new oral or written sentences in which the idioms would seem to make sense. The full class can compare and discuss the new contexts. For example: *ride the gravy train:*

Team 1: She's been *riding the gravy train* ever since she got her allowance.

Team 2: When you're broke, you can't *ride the gravy train*.

Team 3: My sister *rides the gravy train* because all the rest of us do her work.

Through the discussion, the class might conclude that to *ride the gravy train* means to have a soft life or to not have to worry about money.

Artistically inclined students might relish illustrating the incorrect idiomatic meanings—that is, the literal meanings of the words in an idiom.

Such illustrations use contrast to solidify the real meanings of the idioms. Examples could include a picture of a girl on a train with tank cars labeled *gravy*, a picture of children chasing a goose in the outdoors, or a picture of an unhappy looking boy turning on faucets in the sink. The book *101 American English Idioms* (Collis, 1997) includes a "literal," humorous illustration of each idiom, and these could be used to demonstrate this activity.

## *Figures of Speech*

Figures of speech are rhetorical devices that use words in distinctive ways to achieve special effects. They make an impact that is either descriptive, shocking, political, social, upbeat, entertaining, or imaginative. Figurative language is used in contrast to plain or ordinary language; in fact, figurative language may be considered an antonym of literal language. McArthur (1996) identified four types of figures of speech: phonological, orthographic, syntactic, and lexical (p. 368). The two types that occur most often in language use—phonological and lexical—are described and exemplified next.

Phonological figures of speech depend on word sounds to achieve their desired effect. Three phonological figures of speech are alliteration, onomatopoeia, and tongue twisters.

*Alliteration.*    Alliteration is the repetition of initial sounds in contiguous or nearby words. It is most often used to show the range of a subject or to make a contrast (e.g., *Fred was feared from Freedonia, Florida to Freiburg, France*).

*Onomatopoeia.*    Onomatopoeia involves the formation of words from natural sounds (e.g., *choo-choo, oink, quack, kerchoo*) or to suggest sounds (e.g., *Pow! Bang! Crack! Kersplat!*).

*Tongue Twisters.*    Tongue twisters are sentences and phrases that are difficult to pronounce when quickly repeated three or more times (e.g., *red leather yellow leather*).

Lexical figures of speech are expressions that go beyond the literal through the use of exaggeration, diminution, comparison, or some other association. Eleven lexical figures of speech are highlighted here.

*Similes.*    Similes are fanciful or less-than-realistic comparisons that include the words *like* or *as* (e.g., That proverb is *as old as the hills*; it can be traced to ancient times. Dennis has a *mind like a steel trap*; you cannot outsmart him).

*Metaphors.*    Metaphors are similar to condensed similes. They do not use *like* or *as*. They make a comparison by saying one thing *is* another (e.g., *The faculty were sheep who lolled in the pastures of their offices*).

*Hyperbole.*    Speakers use hyperbole to make exaggerated statements that they do not intend to have taken literally. (For example, Our two tomato plants yielded *tons of tomatoes*. It would take *a hundred lifetimes* to grow them more succulent than ours.)

*Meiosis.*    These figures of speech are the opposite of hyperbole. They are understatements that are used to show something to be less significant than it really is. Sometimes meiosis is used to belittle (e.g., *The only difference between an Ed.D. and a high school diploma is a few more years of boredom*).

*Euphemisms.*    Euphemisms are words or phrases thought to be inoffensive or comforting, which are used as substitutions for painful or taboo words (e.g., "How long has Rod been *gone* now?" instead of "How long has Rod been *dead*?"). The English language abounds with euphemisms, which suggests that we tend to avoid being blatant about things unpleasant. Allan and Burridge (1991) presented a comprehensive treatment in their book *Euphemism and Dysphemism: Language as Shield and Weapon.*

*Dysphemisms.*    This figure of speech involves the use of negative or demeaning words as weapons against others. The expressions are used specifically because their connotations are offensive to the topic or to the audience (e.g., *Loretta is not just thrifty, she is a cheapskate*).

*Doublespeak.*    This figure of speech, identified by the National Council of Teachers of English, refers to language that is used to conceal what actually is meant so that something unpleasant may seem more tolerable. (For example, airlines speak of *personal flotation devices* rather than *life jackets*; businesses may advertise *a new car alternative* rather than *a used car*; people who blind themselves to the realities of life have referred to homeless people as *urban campers*.) The *Quarterly Review of Doublespeak,* published by the National Council of Teachers of English, watches the media and exposes examples of doublespeak.

*Oxymorons.*    Oxymorons are figures of speech that juxtapose words of opposite meanings or that usually would not be used together in a paradoxical expression (e.g., *a cheerful pessimist, to make haste slowly, gourmet hot dogs*).

*Irony.*    In this figure of speech words are used in an opposite manner to their usual meanings for the purpose of sarcasm or humor. (For example, "I'll bet *you're thrilled* you came with me to the concert" meaning "I'll bet *you're sorry* you came with me to this bomb. The dogs are howling at the soloist." "She got the promotion because of her *honesty, independence, and intelligence*" meaning "She got the promotion because she's *the Dean's toady.*")

*Personification.*   When using personification, animals, plants, objects, and ideas are given human qualities. (For example, *The red sun dove into the sea and quickly swam under the waves. That old chair has a soft spot in its heart for Uncle Doug.*)

*Puns.*   Puns are figures of speech in which words of similar spelling, sound, or meanings are substituted for the expected words to create a humorous effect. (For example, *I know my poetry is bad but it could be verse. Time flies like the wind but fruit flies like old bananas.*)

These eleven figures of speech are the most frequently used by speakers and writers who employ such rhetorical devices, but there are many others. Your students might enjoy researching additional figures of speech such as allegory, anachronism, bathos, echoism, litote, synedoch, trope, and zeugma.

### Teaching Suggestions

1. Tongue twisters can be tricky for students of any age. Have your students try the following established tongue twisters. Their task is to say the phrase as fast as possible, three times in a row, without any mispronunciations.

Some good laughs are bound to occur—not at one another's expense, but at the strange sounding pronunciations that result.

a. Rubber baby buggy bumpers . . . (pronounced three times)
b. She sells seashells by the seashore.
c. Mixed biscuits
d. Three free thugs set three thugs free.
e. Black bugs' blood
f. Lemon liniment
g. Cheap ship trips
h. Toy boat
i. A regal rural ruler
j. Which wristwatches are Swiss wristwatches?

Have your students try their hand at creating original tongue twisters to share with the class.

2. Metaphors are comparisons between two unlike objects or ideas. They do not signal the comparison by using the words *like* or *as* as is done with similes. Fiction writers for all ages use metaphors to make subtle comparisons. From the children's books in your room, select sentences containing metaphors. Engage your students in a discussion about what comparisons are being made, what the sentences could mean literally, what the metaphors are intended to mean, and in what context the metaphors would be appropriate. Here are some examples:

   **a.** Kennedy International Airport is the welcome mat to America.
   **b.** Cedric's new sweater is a furnace.
   **c.** Mr. May's cupboards are a pasta factory.
   **d.** Linda's classroom is a rural village at 3:00 A.M.
   **e.** The parade leader's baton was the rotating blade of a rising helicopter.
   **f.** At rush hour the subway is always a stuffed sausage, especially the Green Line.
   **g.** The "day-old" bread was a rock.
   **h.** The local coffee shop is a daily gossip column.

Next, ask your students to try their hand at creating some. Topics such as the following could be used by them in writing prose or poetry:

| | |
|---|---|
| summer dandelions | a year-old calendar |
| a clothes dryer | spaghetti |
| that garbage truck | the first cold day |
| raindrops on the window | the cactus |
| a neon sign | sharks |
| Mars | my telephone |

## Word Associations

Most English words are related to other words in English through some shared semantic element. These word associations correspond both to what the words mean and how the words are stored and accessed in the mental lexicon. Learning new words through their associations with known words takes advantage of an established principle of learning, known as *schema theory* (Rumelhart, 1980).

   Aitchison (1997) used the term *human word-web* to describe the way in which humans organize words in semantic fields. The semantic fields of related words in the mental lexicon enable speakers and writers to instantaneously select the words they need as they communicate. Aitchison (1994) identified five types of word associations (pp. 82–98) and Pearson and Johnson (1978, p. 53) described nine types. The following description of ten kinds of word associations is drawn from both of those sources and from the work of Carter (1987), Crystal (1995), and Miller (1996).

*Synonyms.*   Synonyms are words that are nearly the same or quite similar in meaning (e.g., *small, tiny, petite, diminutive*). No two words have exactly the same meaning in all contexts. There always is some slight difference in frequency, distribution, or connotation of synonyms.

*Panthera leo* and *lion, cucurbit* and *squash, sodium carbonate* and *washing soda* have quite different frequencies in English. We all know that a *house* is not a *home*, . . . that not all *men* are *gentlemen;* at a more subtle level, we soon learn the differences between *motherly* and *maternal, fatherly* and *paternal, brotherly* and *fraternal*. These are connotative differences. (Rodale, 1978, introduction)

The words *interested, curious,* and *nosy* denote the same general meaning, but *curious* and *nosy* have very different connotations. Synonyms are words with semantic similarity.

*Antonyms.*    Antonyms are words that have opposite meanings (e.g., *large-small, old-young, new-used*). Crystal (1995, p. 165) distinguished between three types of antonyms. Gradable antonyms such as *cool* and *warm* exist on a continuum (e.g., *cold, cool, tepid, warm, hot*) and therefore do not represent absolute differences. Complementary antonyms are words that are mutually exclusive. If you are *alive,* you are not *dead*. You either are *married* or *single*. Converse antonyms such as *over* and *under* and *buy* and *sell* are mutually dependent on one another. There cannot be one without the other. These fine-line distinctions could confuse most elementary and middle school students for whom knowing that antonyms are "opposites" probably is quite sufficient.

*Collocations.*    Collocations are words that frequently occur together in language usage (e.g., *commit murder, purple passion, rancid butter*). Words that somewhat habitually occur together lend themselves to joint discussion. Why do we commit a crime but do a job? Why is butter rancid but milk sour, canned food spoiled, and teeth decayed?

*Coordinates.*    Coordinates are words that cluster together on some semantic element but are not superordinate or subordinate to one another. *Cheese, tomato sauce, olives, sausage, onions,* and *pepperoni* are all toppings for a *pizza*. They have equal value in terms of the pizza. Coordinate words are the subordinate words within each of the next four word-association categories.

*Hypernyms-Hyponyms.*    A hypernym is the superordinate word in a category (e.g., *Fruit*), and hyponyms are the subordinate members of the category (e.g., *apples, oranges, bananas*). A hypernym in one category may be a hyponym in another category (e.g., *Food: fruit, vegetables, grains, meat*), and a hyponym can serve as a hypernym of a different category (e.g., *Apples: Jongold, Braeburn, Delicious*). These relationships are shown in the following diagram.

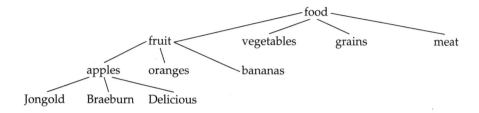

***Hypernyms-Meronyms.*** Meronyms are parts of a whole which is the hypernym (e.g., *Tree: branches, roots, trunk, bark, leaves*). The word "meronomy" was coined by Hasan (1984) to describe part-whole associations between words.

***Hypernyms-Attributes.*** This type of word association describes the relationship between the hypernym and its semantic features (e.g., *Kiwi Fruit: small, sweet, green flesh, brown skin, New Zealand*).

***Hypernyms-Functions.*** Words that describe what the hypernym is used for—what it does or what is done to it—are word function associations (e.g., *Automobile: drive it, repair it, wash it, display it, transportation*). The following diagram illustrates the four categories of word associations described above for the hypernym *Pizza*.

***Pizza***

| *Hyponyms* <br> *(types)* | *Meronyms* <br> *(parts)* | *Attributes* <br> *(features)* | *Functions* <br> *(uses)* |
|---|---|---|---|
| cheese | crust | flat | meals |
| sausage | sauce | hot | dates |
| deluxe | toppings | tasty | parties |
| four-meat | seasonings | fattening | meetings |

***Homographs.*** Homographs are multiple-meaning words that have the same spellings but different meanings (e.g., *swing* on the playground, play *swing* music; *net* a butterfly, *net* worth). Some homographs have different pronunciations as well (e.g., have good *conduct, conduct* the band; a *bow* tie, actors take a *bow*).

***Homophones.*** Homophones are words that have the same sound but different spellings and different meanings (e.g., *pear-pair, brake-break*). The spellings of the homophones signal their different meanings. In oral language, however, only the contextual usage is available to reveal the intended meanings of homophones.

These ten categories of word associations comprise the major elements in our human word webs. Each type of association offers opportunities for word play activities.

### Teaching Suggestions

1. *Making word trees.* Classifying words according to four types of word associations described in this section can be both instructive and challenging. Here is an example of a "starter" word tree for the hypernym *Insects.*

**Insects**

| *Kinds* | *Parts* | *Attributes* | *Functions* |
|---|---|---|---|
| termite | antennae | camouflage | fish bait |
| walking stick | abdomen | jump | eat insects |
| _____ | _____ | _____ | _____ |
| _____ | _____ | _____ | _____ |
| _____ | _____ | _____ | _____ |

Partially completed word trees such as the one above can serve as a guide to conduct research about a topic (hypernym). Discussion of the completed word trees helps solidify students' knowledge of the words so that they can be used in further written or spoken language. In Chapter 1 we discussed words as two-sided coins with meaning and form on one side and sound on the other side. Word trees help to place words within our mental lexicons by semantic fields.

Two books that I have found helpful in selecting word categories for instruction in vocabulary and word play are *The Order of Things: How Everything in the World Is Organized into Hierarchies, Structures, and Pecking Orders* (Kipfer, 1997), and *A Cluster Approach to Elementary Vocabulary Instruction* (Marzano & Marzano, 1988). Both contain hundreds of categories of words. Any topic under discussion in your class or of interest to you or your students will lend itself to this type of classification word play.

2. *Alike and different.* Many pairs of words are alike in one way but different in another. For example, a *flashlight* and a *candle* both give off light, but a *candle* has a flame. A *computer* and a *piano* both have keys, but a *computer* can be used to send e-mail and a *piano* cannot. Discussion of words that are alike but different might center on how the words differ in attributes, functions, parts, types, or on some other basis. The following word pairs could be used to initiate such discussions. Your students will generate others.

| | |
|---|---|
| umbrella-raincoat | fur-wool |
| Chicago-Boston | onion-carrot |
| vinegar-garlic | honey-jelly |
| chalk-crayon | cafeteria-restaurant |
| refrigerator-freezer | apartment-condominium |
| carport-garage | lawn-patio |
| shelves-hangers | hose-pipe |
| lamp-chandelier | farmer-gardener |
| odometer-speedometer | binoculars-telescope |
| discussion-debate | balloon-flute |
| photographer-illustrator | sculptor-potter |
| fable-tall tale | area code-zip code |

Word pairs can be used in word games (e.g., I'm thinking of two words that are sweet and can be spread on bread, but one comes from bees. What are they?).

## Word Formation

Aitchison (1994) used the metaphor "lexical tool kit" to describe the human ability to create new words and the procedures used in the process (p. 131). Most English words have come into existence in one of four ways:

1. through the addition of prefixes and suffixes to existing root words (e.g., *pretest, untie, kindness, Americanism*);
2. by combining words to form compound words (e.g., *storyteller, seashell*);
3. by shortening or abbreviating existing words (e.g., *ETA*—estimated time of arrival, *NOW*—National Organization of Women, *flu*—influenza); and
4. by converting the grammatical function of a word. For example, in the sentences "Charline is an *author*. She has *coauthored* a new text," the noun *author* has been converted to the verb in *coauthored*.

These word formation categories are described and exemplified next.

*Prefixes.* A prefix is an affix that is added at the beginning of a word to form a new word. Most prefixes contribute to the meaning of the new word. Common types of prefixes have to do with number (e.g., *bifocal, triangle, multidimensional*), size (e.g., *minibaguette, megamean*), degree (e.g., *substandard, overworked, underpaid*), order (e.g., *pretest, rewrite*), negation (e.g., *unwell, nonsense*), or reversal (e.g., *disassemble, deice*). Some prefixes have more than one meaning (e.g., *overhead, overcoat*), and some meanings are represented by more than one prefix (e.g., *immoral, illegal, incomprehensible, irrational*).

*Suffixes.*     Suffixes are affixes added to the ends of root words. There are two kinds of suffixes, inflectional and derivational. Inflectional suffixes change the form or grammatical function of the root word but not its basic meaning. Inflectional suffixes indicate tense (e.g., *walks, walking, walked*), comparison (e.g., *long, longer, longest*), plurality (e.g., *team-teams, watch-watches*), possession (e.g., *Carolyn's coat, the girls' coats*), and contractions (e.g., *aren't, they're*). Derivational suffixes, on the other hand, usually change the basic meaning of the root word as well as its grammatical function. For example, the suffix *-ness* changes an adjective to a noun *(stubbornness), -ize* changes a noun to a verb *(harmonize), -able* changes a verb to an adjective *(rideable),* and *-ly, -wards,* and *-wise* are used to create adverbs *(smoothly, downwards, clockwise).*

Some suffixes have gained popularity during a particular era and then have faded into disuse. The suffix *-ville (ho-humsville, dullsville, drabsville)* was in common slang use in the 1950s. The suffix of the 1960s was *-y (grubby, yucky, scuzzy).* The suffix *-o* originated in the 1920s and seems to reappear every couple of decades *(daddyo, wrongo, sicko)* (B. Johnson, 1999). Language users are innately adept at creating new words using existing root words together with appropriate prefixes and suffixes.

*Compounds.*     Compound words are formed by combining two or more other words (e.g., *hambone, daylight*). Miller (1996, pp. 116–117) differentiated two types of compound words, endocentric and exocentric. Endocentric compounds always refer to something named by the final word in the pair (e.g., *doorknob, rainwater, crybaby*). Exocentric compounds refer to something other than the words within the compound (e.g., *mushroom, turnkey, butterfly*). It probably would be more accurate to think of exocentric compounds as "compound-look-alikes" that have separate syllables, not adjoined words.

Compounding is the simplest way to make new words, and most languages, especially German, make use of it. Some compounds are written as one word (e.g., *catfish, bathroom*), others as two words (e.g., *bubble gum, golf course*), and still others are hyphenated (e.g., *safe-conduct, care-free*). How can one be sure that a compound written as two words actually is a compound and not a noun phrase? The test is easy: Noun phrases can take the adverb *very* (e.g., a very old clock, a very green lake), but compound words cannot (e.g., a very bubble gum, or a very golf course). Compound words usually stress the first word, but noun phrases stress the second word (e.g., compare *darkroom* with *dark room*). Compound words can be nouns *(suitcase),* adjectives *(homesick)*, or verbs *(sight-read)*. Compounding is a valuable tool in our lexical tool kits, and new compounds are created continuously.

***Abbreviations.***     Abbreviations are words that have been shortened in some way. They include acronyms, initialisms, F.W.O.s, clippings, and blends.

*Acronyms and Initialisms.*     Both acronyms and initialisms are abbreviations of words formed by using just the first letter (usually) of each word. The difference between the two is that acronyms are pronounceable words (e.g., *BART, VISTA*), but initialisms can be said only as letters (e.g., *ATM, GPA, AI*). Abbreviations form a huge group of words in English. The *Acronyms, Initialisms, and Abbreviations Dictionary* (Gale Research) presents nearly 500,000 entries and is updated annually.

*F.W.O.s.*     The term *F.W.O.s* was coined by B. Johnson (in press) to refer to abbreviations that are used "for writing only." F.W.O.s are not used in spoken language; indeed, it would sound strange to try to use them orally. Examples include: *adj.* (adjective), *govt.* (government), *attn.* (attention), *misc.* (miscellaneous), *tbsp.* (tablespoon), and many others.

*Clippings.*     Clipped words are words that have been shortened through common use. They are abbreviations in which part of the word stands for the whole word. What college student or graduate is not familiar with these clipped words: *econ, lit, phys ed, gym, dorm, el ed, prof, grad,* and *alum?* Clipped words come in all shapes and sizes, and they are a part of everyday use (e.g., *cab, Doc, flu*).

*Blends.*     Blends, also called portmanteau words, are made by combining the abbreviated forms of two or more words. Highly familiar blends include *brunch, smog,* and *motel.* Newer blends such as *bit* (binary + digit), *Chunnel* (Channel + tunnel), *caplet* (capsule + tablet), and *infomercial* (information + commercial) will no doubt be superseded by blends yet to be generated.

*Conversions.*     A final mechanism in our lexical tool kits is what linguists call conversions. To "convert" a word is to change its grammatical function without making any changes to the word. Verbs can be changed to nouns (That poker player is a *cheat*), nouns to verbs (Did you *bottle* that water yet?), adjectives to verbs (Let me help you *dry* the dishes), adjectives to nouns (Did you pass your *final* today?), and nouns to adjectives (It was cooked in a *copper* pan).

Our lexical tool kits enable us to create new words that make sense to other speakers of the language. Word formation is a fertile field for word play, as many school children have discovered.

## Teaching Suggestions

Elementary and middle school students get excited about trying to create new words—words that could exist and maybe even should exist—but are not found in a general dictionary.

The following creative word formations were "unclaimed" on the Internet. Most were made by combining actual words and actual prefixes and suffixes. Share the words, pronunciations, and definitions with your class, and have them use the words in sentences or in little scenarios. Challenge them to create some new words along these lines.

1. *aquadextrous* (ak wa DEKS trus) adj. Possessing the ability to turn the bathtub faucet on and off with your toes.
2. *burgacide* (BURG uh side) n. When a hamburger can't take anymore torture and hurls itself through the grill into the coals.
3. *disconfect* (dis kon FEKT) v. To sterilize the piece of candy you dropped on the floor by blowing on it, somehow assuming this will remove all the germs.
4. *eiffelites* (EYE ful eyetz) n. Gangly people sitting in front of you at the movies who, no matter what direction you lean in, follow suit.
5. *elbonics* (el BON iks) n. The actions of two people maneuvering for one armrest in a movie theater.
6. *elecelleration* (el a cel er AY shun) n. The mistaken notion that the more you press an elevator button the faster it will arrive.
7. *lactomangulation* (LAK to man gyu LAY shun) n. Manhandling the "open here" spout on a milk container so badly that one has to resort to the "illegal" side.
8. *neonphancy* (ne ON fan see) n. A fluorescent light bulb struggling to come to life.
9. *phonesia* (fo NEE zhuh) n. The affliction of dialing a phone number and forgetting whom you were calling just as they answer.
10. *telecrastination* (tel e kras tin AY shun) n. The act of always letting the phone ring at least twice before you pick it up, even when you're only six inches away.

Challenge your students, in teams, to engage in word formation either by adding affixes to root words, compounding, abbreviating, or through conversion. Each new word should be presented like a dictionary entry with pronunciation, part of speech, definition, and sample sentence and, where appropriate, an illustration. For example:

> *otto* (AH toe) v. To propose simplistic solutions to complex problems. The mayor *ottoed* when asked about the crumbling schools.

The new creations can be displayed on posters or shared in some other way with the full class.

## Word Shapes and Spellings

This form of word play involves the manipulation of the shapes or spellings of words, expressions, and longer units of discourse. The following are representative of this type of word play.

*Anagrams.*   To create an anagram, the letters of one or more words are re-arranged to form another word or words (e.g., *add-dad, read-dear, super-purse, recent-center*).

*Aptanagrams.*   Aptanagrams are the rearrangements of letters in a word or words to produce words that are apt or fit the meaning of the original word (e.g., *ocean-canoe, point-on tip*).

*Antigrams.*   A more difficult adaptation of an anagram is the formation of an antigram. Antigrams are new words that have opposite or incongruous meanings of the words being rearranged (e.g., *teach-cheat, funeral-real fun*).

*Lipograms.*   Lipograms are sentences or longer units of writing in which a particular letter is omitted throughout. Lipograms are easy to write omitting *q* and *z* but are more difficult when omitting high-frequency letters such as *t*, *s*, or any of the vowels. Creators of vanity license plates sometimes omit all of the vowels (e.g., *PCKRFN* means *Packer fan*, *BRWNSR1* means *The Browns are number 1*).

*Palindromes.*   These words, phrases, or sentences produce the same sequences when read forward or backward (e.g., *toot; radar; Madam, I'm Adam; Was it a rat I saw?*).

*Semordnilaps.*   These are words that change to other words when they are read backward (e.g., *plug-gulp, loop-pool, desserts-stressed, not now-won ton*).

*Pangrams.*   Pangrams are sentences that are written to include every letter of the alphabet (e.g., *The five boxing wizards jump quickly*).

*Rebuses.*   Rebuses use letters, symbols, numbers, and page arrangements to convey words, common idioms, and other expressions (e.g., ♥ 2 ♥ means *heart to heart*, $\frac{over}{coat}$ means *overcoat*, $\frac{storm}{th}$ means *thunderstorm*, and ↓*town* means *downtown*. Rebuses also are called droodles, pundles, noodles, and other names.

*Formula Puzzles.*    With formula puzzles, a number and the first letters of some missing words are provided. The goal is to identify and write the missing words (e.g., *16 = o.__ in a p.__ means 16 = ounces in a pound, 88 = p.__ k.__ means 88 = piano keys*).

These patterns and procedures are a few of the ways that shapes and spellings of words are altered or rearranged in creative word play. Your students will be able to come up with others.

## Teaching Suggestions

1. Students in grades 3–8 like formula puzzles. Divide your class into pairs or threes and introduce them to the puzzles by using relatively easy ones such as the following:

   | | |
   |---|---|
   | 12 = i.__ in a f.__ | (12 inches in a foot) |
   | 11 = p.__ on a f.__t.__ | (11 players on a football team) |
   | 52 = w.__ in a y.__ | (52 weeks in a year) |
   | 7 = d.__ in a w.__ | (7 days in a week) |

   Each team should attempt to solve as many of the next ten puzzles as they can.

   | | |
   |---|---|
   | 1001 = A.__ N.__ | (1001 Arabian Nights) |
   | 12 = s.__ of the z.__ | (12 signs of the zodiac) |
   | 54 = c.__ in a d.__ with the j.__ | (54 cards in a deck with the jokers) |
   | 9 = p.__ in the s.__ s.__ | (9 planets in the solar system) |
   | 32 = d.__ F.__ at which w.__ f.__ | (32 degrees Fahrenheit at which water freezes) |
   | 200 = d.__ for p.__ g.__ in M.__ | (200 dollars for passing go in *Monopoly*) |
   | 90 = d.__ in a r.__ a.__ | (90 degrees in a right angle) |
   | 3 = b.__ m.__, s.__ h.__ t.__ r.__ | (3 blind mice, see how they run) |
   | 4 = q.__ in a g.__ | (4 quarts in a gallon) |
   | 29 = d.__ in F.__ in a l.__ y.__ | (29 days in February in a leap year) |

   Encourage the teams to try to create one or two similar puzzles to use with the class.

2. Anagrams have been a source of word play enjoyment since "they were invented by the Greek poet Lycophron in 260 B.C." (Begerson,

1973, p. 40). Any activity that has been popular for more than 2,200 years has some enduring quality. An anagram is a new word formed by rearranging the letters in a word (e.g., *rate-tear*).

Anagrams are not always easy for elementary and middle grade students. One way to help students is to provide a semantic clue to the meaning of the anagram as shown in the following examples.

| *Original Word* | *Clue Word* | *Anagram* |
|---|---|---|
| last | seasoning | salt |
| stun | cashews | nuts |
| seals | lower prices | sales |
| edit | eat less | diet |
| chain | good dishes | china |
| den | the finish | end |
| tool | money | loot |
| gasp | spaces | gaps |
| slope | north and south | poles |
| scrub | street edges | curbs |

Save the clue words to use as hints if your students are stumped by the anagrams.

## Word Games

> Word games . . . provide the clearest example of the lengths to which people are prepared to go to indulge in strange linguistic behavior. We take considerable enjoyment from pulling words apart and reconstituting them in some novel guise, arranging them into clever patterns, finding hidden meanings in them, and trying to use them according to specially invented rules. (Crystal, 1995, p. 396)

Are you the type who can't wait to find time to do the daily crossword puzzle? Is an evening of *Scrabble* or *Scategories* your idea of a good time? If so, you are among the millions who like to play word games. Individuals have created word games at least since the beginnings of written language some six thousand years ago, and probably since the earliest stages of oral language. Part of the popularity of word games is their simplicity. Many require only voices or paper and pencil. Games involve, variously, playing with the sounds, shapes, spellings, or meanings of words either in isolation or in context. Most word games can be played by any number of players.

My favorite source of word games is *The Oxford A to Z of Word Games* (Augarde, 1994). This collection presents more than 250 word games and for each game explains the object and procedure, indicates the number of players required, describes the type of game it is, tells whether it is played by writing or speaking, and lists the equipment needed. Examples, background information, and synonymous names for games sometimes are provided. Augarde (pp. xvi–xx) has identified sixteen categories of word games. The following is a list of each category, the number of games in that category, and an example game title for each category.

*Augarde's Sixteen Categories of Word Games*

| Category | Number of Games | Example |
|---|---|---|
| Active | 6 | Charades |
| Alphabetical | 13 | Alphabet Dinner |
| Anagrams | 16 | Countdown |
| Challenge | 67 | Earth, Air, Water |
| Cumulative | 38 | Good News, Bad News |
| Grid Games | 25 | Word Battleships |
| Guessing | 69 | Rebus |
| Letters | 9 | Acronyms |
| Miming | 4 | Dumb Crambo |
| Poetic | 2 | Enigma |
| Punning | 16 | Knock-Knock |
| Rhyming | 3 | Stinky Pinky |
| Spelling | 4 | Spelling Round |
| Word-Building | 15 | Trigrams |
| Word-Finding | 37 | Guggenheim |
| Word Play | 7 | Oxymorons |

Some games in the collection fit into more than one category. For example, "Charades" is listed as an Active game, a Guessing game, and a Miming game. "I packed my bag" is both an Alphabetical game and a Cumulative game. Another major collection of word games, *Masters' Word Game Collection* (Kohl, 1994), describes and exemplifies nine categories of word play. It includes an annotated list of related books as well as thirty pages of teaching ideas.

## Teaching Suggestions

**1.** The *Brain Train* is a game of hink pinks that is based on the age-old, brain-teasing little riddles that have gone by the names stinky pinkies, hank panks, sticklers, and others. Each answer to a short riddle or question is two rhyming words of a specified number of syllables. For example, the answer to "What could you call a weak escargot?" (hink pink) is "a frail snail." The answer to "What might you call a loud boom box that you can hear through the wall?" (hinky pinky) is a "plaster blaster."

References to these riddles are found in Espy (1975), Pearson and Johnson (1978), Brandreth (1980), Burns and Weston (1981), and a number of other sources. The name and date of the original creator of hink pinks is unknown, but many septuagenarians remember playing with these riddles when they were children.

Johnson and Johnson (1994) expanded the number and kinds of hink pink riddles by presenting nine categories of the riddles in three "families" as shown in the following list.

### Hink Pink Family

*Hink pinks* are one-syllable rhyming words used to answer a riddle. "Who is a person who steals steaks?" "a beef thief"

*Hinky pinkies* are two-syllable rhyming words. "What could we call a better cafe?" "a finer diner"

*Hinkety pinketies* are three-syllable rhyming words. "What is it called when you get the O.K. to take something away?" "removal approval"

### Hink Hink Family

*Hink hinks* are one-syllable words that have the same sound and spelling but different meanings. "Which piece of furniture does the head of the committee use?" "the chair chair"

*Hinky hinkies* are two-syllable words that have the same sound and spelling but different meanings. "What could we call an intestinal punctuation mark?" "a colon colon"

*Hinkety hinketies* are three-syllable words that have the same sound and spelling but different meanings. "What do call a round handbill?" "a circular circular"

### Pink Pink Family

*Pink pinks* are one-syllable words that have the same sound but a different spelling and a different meaning. "What is a self-centered blood vessel called?" "a vain vein"

*Pinky pinkies* are two-syllable words that have the same sound but a different spelling and a different meaning. "Who talks rhythmically to music about the paper around a candy bar?" "a wrapper rapper"

*Pinkety pinketies* are three-syllable words that have the same sound but a different spelling and a different meaning. "What might you call the main rule?" "the principal principle"

The *Brain Train* game is played by two teams (the "Shrewd Brood" and the "Quick Clique") of any size and a moderator (the "Big Wig") who poses the riddle questions. The moderator tells which of the nine categories will be used and then asks the question. Teams are given fifteen seconds to decide on an answer. To avoid confusion, only one team member (the "Choice Voice") can speak for the team. The "Big Wig" calls on the "Choice Voice" whose hand goes up first. If the team's answer is correct, the team scores two points. If the answer is incorrect, the other team gets a chance at it for one point. If neither team gets it correct, the players are given a clue (i.e., first letters of each word). A correct answer then gets the team one point. When neither team answers correctly, they each get a zero. Ten riddle questions constitute a game, and the team with the most points wins. The *Brain Train* may be adapted in several ways (e.g., using only hink pinks or just a few of the nine categories, or by providing semantic clues, or by allowing more than fifteen seconds to reach agreement on an answer). The game has been popular with students in fifth grade and above and with younger children when only easier hink pinks or hinky pinkies are used. Analyzing the game according to Augarde's sixteen categories indicates that the *Brain Train* would qualify as a Challenge game, a Rhyming game, and a Spelling game.

Many elementary and middle schoolers like to create their own hink pink riddles. Creating and solving such riddles enhances critical thinking and problem solving, expands vocabularies, and develops interest in language in addition to providing engaging word play.

**2.** *Twenty Questions* was a popular radio game show in the 1940s and 1950s. It is played by two or more players. The first player thinks of a word and tells whether the word is "animal, vegetable, or mineral." The other players then may ask up to a total of twenty questions to try to guess the word. The questions must be formed so that they can be answered with a yes or no. The category "animal" refers to humans, animals, or something from an animal (e.g., *antlers*). "Vegetable" refers to plants and their by-products (e.g., *beans, books*). "Mineral" designates any inorganic object (e.g., *spoon, diamond*). The first person to guess the correct word gets to select the next target word, and the game continues. For example, the following is a transcript of a game played by three players.

Player 1 says that he is thinking of a word that is "animal."

P2:   Is it a person?
P1:   No.
P3:   Is it living?
P1:   Yes.
P2:   Is there one in this town?
P1:   No.
P3:   Is there one in America?
P1:   Yes.
P2:   Is this animal usually a pet?
P1:   No.
P3:   Would you find it in a zoo?

P1:  Yes.

P2:  Does it have fur?

P1:  Yes.

P3:  Does it have spots?

P1:  Yes.

P2:  It's a leopard, isn't it?

P1:  Yes, you win!

Next, Player 2, the winner, gets to select a word.

Brandreth (1980) described his feelings about words and, in so doing, captured my own.

> I'm a word freak. I'm fascinated by language, the way we use it and abuse it, the way we can manipulate it and be manipulated by it, the tricks we can play with it, the marvels we can create with it, the sheer fun we can have with it. (introduction)

Teachers who help their students capture the sheer fun that can be had with words will see them well on their way to continued growth in vocabulary and expanded command of the English language.

Our lexical journey is complete. We have explored the intricacies of what words are. We have visited a number of word-play mechanisms that can help stimulate or maintain interest in language. We have seen ways vocabulary grows through listening and speaking. We have examined the criticality of word knowledge to reading comprehension, and we have witnessed the essentiality of using just the right words when writing. We have opened the covers of thesauri and dictionaries and made the acquaintance of electronic resources for vocabulary. We have experienced the wonder of words and words used well. And we have taken a quick peek at the complexities surrounding vocabulary testing. It is my hope that you have deemed the journey worthwhile and that your interest in words has been sustained. If some of the suggestions herein find their way into your classroom, I will be gratified.

## References

Aitchison, J. (1994). *Words in the mind: An introduction to the mental lexicon* (2nd ed.). Oxford, UK: Blackwell.

Aitchison, J. (1997). *The language web.* Cambridge, UK: Cambridge University Press.

Allan, K., & Burridge, K. (1991). *Euphemism & dysphemism: Language used as shield and weapon.* New York: Oxford University Press.

Ash, R. (1995). *The top 10 of everything: 1996.* New York: Dorling Kindersley.

Augarde, T. (1994). *The Oxford a to z of word games.* Oxford, UK: Oxford University Press.

Bergerson, H. W. (1973). *Palindromes and anagrams.* New York: Dover Publications, Inc.

Brandreth, G. (1980). *The joy of lex.* New York: William Morrow.

Brent, H. (Ed.). (April, 1998). *Quarterly Review of Doublespeak*. Urbana, IL: National Council of Teachers of English.

Burns, M., & Weston, M. (1981). *The hink pink book*. Boston: Little, Brown and Company.

Carter, R. (1987). *Vocabulary: Applied linguistic perspectives*. New York: Routledge.

Collis, H. (1997). *101 American English idioms*. Lincolnwood, IL: Passport Books.

Crystal, D. (1995). *The Cambridge encyclopedia of the English language*. Cambridge, UK: Cambridge University Press.

Dickson, P. (1996). *What's in a name? Reflections of an irrepressible name collector*. Springfield, MA: Merriam-Webster, Inc.

Douglas, A. (1990). *Webster's New World dictionary of eponyms*. New York: Webster's New World.

Dunn, J. (1997). *Idiom savant: Slang as it is slung: The colorful lingo of American subcultures, from animators to zine readers*. New York: Henry Holt and Company.

Espy, W. R. (1975). *An almanac of words at play*. New York: Clarkson N. Potter, Inc.

Flavell, L., & Flavell, R. (1993). *Dictionary of proverbs and their origins*. New York: Barnes & Noble Books.

Geller, L. G. (1985). *Wordplay and language learning for children*. Urbana, IL: National Council of Teachers of English.

Golick, M. (1987). *Playing with words*. Markham, ON: Pembroke Publishers Limited.

Hanks, P., & Hodges, F. (1988). *A dictionary of surnames*. Oxford, UK: Oxford University Press.

Hanks, P., & Hodges, F. (1990). *A dictionary of first names*. Oxford, UK: Oxford University Press.

Hasan, R. (1984). Coherence and cohesive harmony. In J. Flood (Ed.), *Understanding reading comprehension* (pp. 181–219). Newark, DE: International Reading Association.

Johnson, B. v. H. (in press). *Word works: Exploring language play*. Golden, CO: Fulcrum Publishing.

Johnson, D. D., & Johnson, B. v. H. (1994). *The brain train*. Elizabethtown, PA: Continental Press.

Kipfer, B. A. (1997, 1998). *The order of things: How everything in the world is organized into hierarchies, structures, and pecking orders*. New York: Random House.

Kohl, H. (1994). *Masters' word game collection*. New York: Barnes & Noble Books.

Lighter, J. E. (Ed.). (1994). *Random House historical dictionary of American slang* (Vol. 1). New York: Random House.

Marzano, R. J., & Marzano, J. S. (1988). *A cluster approach to elementary vocabulary instruction*. Newark, DE: International Reading Association.

McArthur, T. (Ed.). (1996). *The concise Oxford companion to the English language*. Oxford, UK: Oxford University Press.

Miller, G. A. (1996). *The science of words*. New York: Scientific American Library.

Pearson, P. D., & Johnson, D. D. (1978). *Teaching reading comprehension*. New York: Holt, Rinehart and Winston.

Rees, N. (1995). *Dictionary of catchphrases*. London, UK: Cassell Publishers Limited.

Rodale, J. I. (1978). *The synonym finder*. New York: Warner Books.

Rumelhart, D. E. (1980). Schemata: The building blocks of cognition. In R. J. Spiro, B. C. Bruce, & W. F. Brewer (Eds.)., *Theoretical issues in reading comprehension*. Hillsdale, NJ: Erlbaum.

Spears, R. A. (1998). *NTC's thematic dictionary of American idioms*. Lincolnwood, IL: NTC Publishing Group.

Terban, M. (1996). *Scholastic dictionary of idioms*. New York: Scholastic.

U.S. Department of Education. (1987). *What works: Research about teaching and learning* (2nd ed.). Washington, D.C.: Author.

# *Author Index*

# Subject Index